When You're the One They Ask

A Partner's Guide to OCD, Family Accommodation, and How to Stop Helping in the Ways That Make It Worse

Ruby Virginia Barman

Book 3 of 3

This book is for general educational and informational purposes. It explains research and practical concepts related to obsessive-compulsive disorder, family accommodation, relationships, and support. It is not a diagnostic tool and does not replace individualized medical or mental-health care.
No book can determine whether a particular thought, behavior, conflict, or safety concern is caused by OCD. A qualified clinician can assess symptoms in context. Decisions about diagnosis, exposure and response prevention, psychotherapy, medication, or changes to prescribed treatment belong with appropriately qualified professionals and the person receiving care.
The reader remains responsible for decisions about personal safety, children, finances, housing, legal matters, and relationships. If there is immediate danger, a credible threat of violence, a medical emergency, risk of self-harm, or concern about a dependent person's safety, use appropriate emergency or professional services rather than applying a self-help rule.
Names and scenarios in this book are composites created to illustrate common patterns. They do not describe identifiable individuals. Similarities to real people are coincidental.

ISBN: 978-1-911838-43-2

Table Of Contents

Preface

Family accommodation has become one of the clearest ways researchers describe what obsessive-compulsive disorder can ask of the people around it. The term covers changes made by relatives or partners to reduce OCD-related distress, such as giving repeated reassurance, taking part in rituals, doing checks for someone else, facilitating avoidance, or changing ordinary routines. A 2024 systematic review and meta-analysis brought together 108 studies involving 8,928 people with OCD and found a moderate positive association between family accommodation and OCD symptom severity. The same review also found that accommodation tends to decrease during both individual and family-focused cognitive behavioral treatment. Those findings do not prove that every accommodating act causes more severe OCD, but they do make accommodation an important part of the clinical picture. (Hermida-Barros et al., 2024)

The word *accommodation* can sound colder than the behavior it describes. Much of it begins as care. A partner answers a frightening question because an answer seems kinder than silence. A spouse checks the stove because leaving the house matters more than debating who should check it. Someone changes the laundry routine because the evening has already been consumed by distress. The immediate result can be relief for both people. The long-term difficulty is that a household may begin treating certainty, ritual completion, or avoidance as requirements.

This book focuses on the romantic partner's position inside that pattern. It uses one organizing method, the Support Pivot: notice the pattern, meet the person, decline the accommodation, and return the next choice. The method is not a home version of exposure and response prevention. It is a way for a partner to decide what *their own* response will be when OCD pulls for certainty, checking, participation, or a rule change. Where a treatment plan already gives the partner a specific role, that plan takes priority.

This is the third book in a three-book series, but it stands on its own. Its narrow job is to address family accommodation from the partner's side, including reassurance loops, delegated checking, household rules, treatment refusal, relationship-centered doubt, children and relatives, conflict, safety, and the partner's own shrinking life. A parent, sibling, or close friend may find parts useful, but the examples and decisions are written for spouses and long-term partners.

The book does not ask you to decide whether every difficult behavior is "the OCD," and it does not give a blanket instruction to stop reassuring someone you love. Ordinary relationship reassurance, comfort after bad news, repair after conflict, and practical safety checks are part of human life. The task is to recognize repetitive certainty-seeking and ritual participation by function, then respond with enough precision that care remains while compulsive assistance decreases. For diagnosis, treatment design, medication questions, crisis concerns, or unclear safety issues, professional help is the appropriate next step.

The purpose here is practical: to help you stop doing the work OCD keeps assigning you while remaining recognizably yourself in the relationship.

Introduction: The Help That Started With Love

Maya was already wearing her coat when Daniel asked whether she had seen him turn off the stove.

"Yes," she said.

He stood in the hall for another few seconds. "All four knobs?"

"All four."

They reached the elevator. Daniel stopped the door with his hand. "You actually looked at them, though?"

Maya could feel the shape of the evening changing. Their reservation was in twenty minutes. She pictured the long walk back down the corridor, the pause in the kitchen, the photograph Daniel sometimes took of the knobs, and the second photograph when the first did not feel clear enough. So she said what had worked before.

"I'll go check."

That sentence was loving in intention. It was also doing a job that belonged to Daniel's OCD.

The hard thing about family accommodation is that it rarely announces itself as a clinical problem. It arrives as a favor. It looks like speed, kindness, peacekeeping, flexibility, or a reasonable compromise for a bad day. Sometimes it really is one of those things. The question is not whether you have ever helped your partner feel better. The question is whether your response has become part of a repeating process in which distress leads to your participation, your participation brings short relief, and the next request returns.

Clinical guidance takes this pattern seriously. NICE recommends that when family members or carers have become involved in compulsive behavior, avoidance, or reassurance seeking, treatment plans should help them reduce that involvement in a sensitive and supportive way. The International OCD Foundation likewise advises families to minimize participation in compulsions and to discuss limits ahead of conflict when possible. (National Institute for Health and Care Excellence, 2005; Van Noppen & Pato, 2009)

That sounds straightforward on paper. At home, it is anything but straightforward.

You may know the request is repetitive and still hate the look on your partner's face when you refuse. You may have tried saying "I won't reassure you" only to discover that the next twenty minutes became an argument about whether the feared event was actually possible. You may be dealing with rules that affect children, shared money, sex, travel, sleep, food, or who can enter the house. You may also have a partner who does not want treatment, has had poor treatment, cannot access specialist care, or believes that *you* are the unreasonable one.

This book starts where those complications start.

Support Is Not the Same as Participation

The central distinction is between supporting a person and performing a function for OCD.

Support responds to the person: "I can see this is hard." "I'll sit with you while the wave passes." "Do you want company on the walk?" "We can talk about what your therapist asked you to practice."

Accommodation responds to the demand for certainty or ritual completion: "Yes, I promise that means you're safe." "I'll check one more time." "Nobody will touch that chair." "I'll cancel the visit so you don't have to feel contaminated." "Tell me the whole thought again and I'll tell you what it says about you."

The same sentence can even serve different functions in different moments. "Of course I love you" may be an ordinary answer in one conversation and the twentieth reassurance in a relationship-OCD loop in another. Function matters more than vocabulary.

That is why a rigid rule such as *never reassure* is too blunt for a relationship. The book will teach you to look for pattern markers: repetition, urgency, temporary relief, escalating precision, inability to let an answer stand, and requests that transfer responsibility for uncertainty to you.

The Support Pivot

When you spot the pattern, use four moves.

First, **notice the pattern**. Ask what the request is doing rather than whether the fear is true. Is this a normal question, a practical check, a request for comfort, or another attempt to obtain certainty?

Second, **meet the person**. Acknowledge distress without certifying the feared conclusion. Warmth and a limit can occupy the same sentence.

Third, **decline the accommodation**. Do not perform the check, answer the repeated certainty question, change the routine, or complete the ritual you have chosen to reduce.

Fourth, **return the next choice**. Hand responsibility back without punishment. That might mean following an agreed treatment plan, making an ordinary decision, tolerating uncertainty for the moment, or choosing what to do next with the evening.

The Support Pivot is about your behavior. It is not a method for controlling your partner's behavior.

Start With One Target, Not the Whole House

A family can be accommodating in dozens of small ways. Trying to eliminate all of them at once can turn every room into a confrontation. Research shows a meaningful association between accommodation and symptom severity, but that evidence does not justify a home campaign in which the partner suddenly withdraws every form of help. A small preliminary randomized trial found benefit when a brief family intervention targeting accommodation was added to individual ERP, but the study included only eighteen patient-family pairs. Its results support the relevance of accommodation reduction, not a claim that abrupt partner-led change is universally effective. (Thompson-Hollands et al., 2015)

The practical rule in this book is *graded reduction*. You will map what you do, choose one accommodation target, make the new response clear, and observe your own consistency. You will not score your partner's anxiety as proof that you are succeeding. You will not turn yourself into an untrained exposure therapist.

Keep a Safety Screen

OCD can attach to real-world subjects: health, driving, appliances, children, money, sex, violence, religion, and morality. That does not make every concern in those areas an OCD request. If you smell gas, you follow a normal safety procedure. If a child may be at risk, you act. If there is a credible threat of violence, you prioritize safety. If a medication question has real clinical consequences, you contact the appropriate professional. Chapter 15 gives you a simple safety screen so that "do not accommodate" never becomes "ignore reality."

What You Are Trying to Restore

The goal is not a perfectly non-accommodating household. It is a household in which OCD has less authority over shared decisions and the partner has more room to be a partner.

You will learn to measure progress from your side. Did you answer once instead of nine times? Did you refuse a delegated check without conducting a courtroom debate? Did the family use the kitchen according to ordinary preferences rather than contamination rules? Did you go to work, sleep in your own bed, meet a friend, or let the children have a normal plan even though OCD objected?

Those are not small questions. They describe whether the relationship still contains two lives.

Before Chapter 1, write down three things you currently do to make OCD-related distress end faster. Do not judge them. Do not change them tonight. For now, you are collecting the information the rest of the book will use.

Part I: See the Pattern

Chapter 1: The Question That Comes Back

Daniel's first question at the restaurant was ordinary enough.

"Did you lock the car?"

Maya said yes. She had driven, parked, locked it, and heard the chirp.

Two minutes later he asked whether she had noticed the lights flash. Then whether the trunk had been fully closed. Then whether she had tried the handle. By the time their food arrived, Maya was not answering a question about a car. She was being asked to become the final authority on a feeling of uncertainty that no answer had settled.

She knew this because every answer produced the same sequence: a pause, a little relief, and then a more precise version of the doubt.

The first skill in this book is to recognize that sequence.

A Question Can Be a Behavior

Reassurance can be part of ordinary intimacy. Partners ask each other whether an outfit looks right, whether a child is okay after a fall, whether a difficult conversation went badly, whether a sound downstairs matters, whether the other person is still angry. Human beings borrow perspective from one another.

Excessive reassurance seeking is different because the answer is asked to do more than provide information or connection. It is asked to remove uncertainty.

In a study of 140 adults with OCD, nearly half reported interpersonal reassurance seeking related to their obsessions. Reassurance seeking was closely related to checking, though the researchers treated the two as distinct behaviors. (Starcevic et al., 2012) Another study comparing self-reported reassurance patterns found that people with OCD described immediate relief after reassurance followed by later return of discomfort and urges to seek reassurance again. The authors cautioned that the work relied on retrospective self-report, so it should not be read as a laboratory proof of every reassurance loop. It does describe the pattern many couples recognize. (Salkovskis & Kobori, 2015)

The useful question for a partner is therefore not, "Is reassurance bad?"

It is, "What is this reassurance doing right now?"

If it gives ordinary information that can stand, you may be having an ordinary conversation. If the answer must be repeated, strengthened, reworded, defended, or guaranteed, you may be inside a certainty loop.

Four Signs the Answer Is Not the Point

Repetition is the first sign. The same question returns after it has been answered, or a new question arrives that serves the same function. "Did you lock it?" becomes "Did you actually pull the handle?" The content moves, but the job stays the same.

Escalating precision is the second. A simple answer is no longer enough. Your partner needs the exact wording, exact probability, exact memory, exact facial expression, or exact sequence of events. The standard for certainty rises as you meet it.

Temporary relief is the third. You can see the question work for a moment. Shoulders drop. The conversation moves on. Then the doubt reappears. Relief is not proof that the answer was harmful, but repeated short relief followed by renewed asking is useful information about function.

Responsibility transfer is the fourth. The question begins to make you responsible for what cannot be guaranteed. "Tell me I didn't offend her" asks you to know another person's internal state. "Promise I won't get sick" asks you to control the future. "Tell me this thought means nothing" asks you to deliver a moral verdict. You are no longer offering perspective. You are being made the holder of certainty.

None of these signs diagnoses OCD. They help you decide whether a familiar interaction is functioning like reassurance seeking in a relationship where OCD is already part of the picture.

Content Pulls You Into Court

The hardest reassurance questions often sound answerable.

"Was that bump in the road a person?"

"Do you think the chicken was cooked?"

"Would you still love me if I had that thought?"

"Are you sure I didn't send the wrong file?"

"Does this symptom look serious?"

Each question invites evidence. You remember the road. You inspect the chicken. You reconstruct the email. You compare the symptom to yesterday. You explain the difference between a thought and an intention.

For a few minutes, the conversation can feel productive because both of you are working hard.

Then OCD discovers the appeal process.

What if you did not see the whole road? What if the thermometer was wrong? What if your interpretation of the thought is too generous? What if the email program sent an old attachment? What if the symptom changed since you looked?

A certainty debate has no natural endpoint because ordinary life rarely provides the standard of proof being demanded. More evidence can create more surfaces to doubt.

This is why the canonical phrase in this book is **process not proof**. When you recognize a reassurance loop, respond to the process of repeated certainty seeking rather than litigating the content of the fear.

That does not mean saying, "That's just OCD," every time your partner raises a concern. That phrase can become dismissive, and it can be wrong. It means noticing when a subject has already received a reasonable answer and the conversation is now trying to erase uncertainty.

First Answer and Repeat Answer

A useful distinction is between a first answer and a repeat answer.

Suppose Elena asks Jonah, "Did I sound rude to your sister at dinner?"

Jonah thinks for a moment. "No. You were direct about leaving early, but I didn't hear you say anything rude."

That may be normal relationship feedback. It contains information Jonah genuinely has.

Ten minutes later Elena asks, "But you didn't see her face after I said it. What if she thought I was angry?"

Jonah now has a choice. He could add more evidence. He could message his sister. He could promise Elena that nobody was offended. Or he could notice that the request has shifted from feedback to certainty.

A process response might be: "I answered what I noticed. I don't want to keep checking whether it was perfect."

If Elena asks again, Jonah does not need a cleverer sentence. Repetition on his side can become its own ritual. He can say, "Same answer. I'm not going to solve it again."

The aim is not to withhold love. The aim is to stop converting love into repeated proof.

Relationship Reassurance Needs More Care

Questions about the relationship itself deserve special attention because a blanket refusal can injure ordinary connection.

Partners should be able to ask, "Are we okay after that argument?" or "Do you still want this relationship?" Those questions can be direct bids for repair. Chapter

12 will deal specifically with relationship-centered obsessions and repetitive certainty seeking.

For now, use one test: **Can the answer stand?**

If your partner can hear an answer, perhaps discuss it once, and then use that information, the exchange may be ordinary. If the answer immediately creates a demand for stronger certainty, new evidence, repeated confession, comparison, or another test of your feelings, look at the process.

You do not need to deny genuine relationship problems to refuse a reassurance loop. Both can be true. "We do need to talk about how we fought yesterday, and I am not going to answer whether we're definitely right for each other twenty times tonight."

That sentence keeps a real problem in the room without letting certainty seeking take the meeting over.

The Cost to Both Partners

Reassurance is often discussed as though only the person asking is affected. In a couple, the giver learns a pattern too.

You learn which answer ends the conversation fastest. You learn when to soften facts. You learn which topics are dangerous to raise before bed. You may begin preemptively checking so the question never arrives. You may take photographs, save receipts, keep messages, remember exact times, or monitor your own expressions because you know they may become evidence later.

The household starts building a second memory system around OCD.

This can make resentment confusing. You may resent the questions and still answer them. You may resent being responsible and still grab responsibility because the alternative is twenty more minutes of distress. You may feel guilty for resenting someone who is genuinely frightened.

There is no need to solve that emotional contradiction before changing your behavior. You can understand why the request is happening and still decide not to serve the same function.

A Forty-Eight-Hour Reassurance Log

Do not begin by refusing every question. Begin by seeing what happens.

For the next forty-eight hours, keep a brief log of reassurance interactions. Record the time, the subject, whether it was the first ask or a repeat ask, what you did, and what happened next. Do not ask your partner to participate in the log unless that would be welcome. This is a record of *your* behavior.

Time	Subject	First or repeat ask	What I did	What happened next
7:40 a.m.	Stove	Repeat	Checked it myself	Left home, asked again in car
1:15 p.m.	Work email	First	Gave ordinary feedback once	Conversation ended
10:05 p.m.	Relationship	Repeat	Explained for 15 minutes	New wording of same question

At the end, circle one interaction with three features: it happened more than once, your answer brought only short relief, and you were asked to guarantee something you could not truly guarantee.

That interaction is a candidate for an **accommodation target**. It is not yet a command to change it. You are learning where the loop has a handle.

What to Say Before You Have a Plan

You may notice the pattern before you and your partner have agreed on a new response. You still need something better than arguing.

Use a temporary process sentence.

"I think we've reached the repeat part of this question. I gave you my answer."

"I care that you're distressed. I don't have more certainty to add."

"I can talk with you about how hard the doubt feels. I don't want to keep proving the answer."

"I answered once. I'm going back to what we were doing."

Notice what these sentences do not contain. They do not call the fear ridiculous. They do not declare that your partner is manipulating you. They do not promise that everything is safe. They also do not open a new courtroom.

Keep the sentence short. Long explanations create material for the next question.

If Your Partner Says You Are Withholding Reassurance on Purpose

They may be right about the first half. You are changing a response deliberately.

The relevant question is *why*.

A punishing refusal says, "Since you won't stop this, you get nothing from me."

A supportive limit says, "I don't want to keep doing the repeated answer because I think it has become part of the loop. I am still here."

Your tone does not have to be perfect. You can be tired. You can be annoyed. You can repair later if you sound sharper than you intended. The standard is not saintly calm. The standard is that the limit is about what you will do, not about making distress disappear faster or teaching your partner a lesson.

In a Nutshell

A reassurance question becomes clinically relevant to the partner when you stop looking only at what it asks and start looking at what the answer is being asked to accomplish.

Repeated asking, escalating precision, short-lived relief, and responsibility transfer are the main markers. When they cluster, use **process not proof**. Give ordinary information when ordinary information is what is needed. When the same demand for certainty returns, notice the process instead of producing a stronger case.

For now, do not change the whole pattern. Complete the forty-eight-hour log. Find one loop you can describe without blame.

In Chapter 2, you will place that loop inside the larger map of family accommodation and see how many forms "helping" can take.

Chapter 2: When Helping Becomes Accommodation

Priya and Marcus had stopped calling it a laundry rule.

It was simply how laundry worked now. Marcus loaded the machine because Priya could not touch clothes that had been on public transport. He ran an extra rinse because detergent residue felt contaminated. He moved clean clothes from washer to dryer because Priya worried her hands would undo the wash. If a sock fell on the floor, he washed the load again.

No single change had felt large enough to fight about. The system had grown one concession at a time.

When Marcus finally counted the steps, he realized that an ordinary household task had become a ritual performed by two people.

That is family accommodation.

The Clinical Idea Without the Blame

In OCD research, family accommodation refers to changes other people make in response to OCD symptoms. It can include participating in rituals, helping with avoidance, modifying routines, providing reassurance, or taking over responsibilities. Reviews have found accommodation to be common and associated with greater OCD symptom severity and functional impairment. (Albert et al., 2017; Wu et al., 2016)

The association is important, but the wording matters.

Accommodation is not a character flaw in the partner. It is not evidence that you caused OCD. It is not proof that you are weak, permissive, codependent, or secretly invested in your partner staying unwell.

It is a behavior pattern.

That distinction is useful because behavior can be mapped and changed without turning the relationship into a moral trial.

The evidence also needs to be stated carefully. Meta-analyses have found a moderate positive correlation between family accommodation and OCD severity. The 2015 meta-analysis by Strauss and colleagues included fourteen studies and 849 participants, with a pooled correlation of .35. A 2016 meta-analysis of forty-one studies found an overall correlation of .42. A larger 2024 review of 108 studies again found a correlation of .42. Correlation does not establish that accommodation is the sole cause of greater symptoms. More severe OCD can also create more pressure for accommodation. (Strauss et al., 2015; Wu et al., 2016; Hermida-Barros et al., 2024)

So the responsible conclusion is not "your helping made your partner sick."

It is "your involvement is part of the system worth changing."

Five Forms of Accommodation

Accommodation becomes easier to see when you stop looking only for reassurance.

Reassurance means providing repeated certainty, moral clearance, memory confirmation, safety guarantees, or relationship proof.

Participation means doing part of a ritual with or for your partner. You may wash, count, repeat, confess, inspect, arrange, photograph, or say a required phrase.

Delegated checking means taking over a check or certifying that it has been completed so responsibility transfers to you.

Facilitated avoidance means changing plans so your partner does not encounter a feared trigger. You drive a longer route, cancel a visit, remove objects, make excuses, or handle tasks they avoid.

Routine modification means reorganizing shared life around OCD rules. Rooms become off-limits. Meals require unusual sequences. Bedtime waits for rituals. Children follow contamination rules. Travel becomes constrained by certainty procedures.

These categories overlap. The purpose of naming them is not to force every act into one box. It is to reveal that accommodation can hide inside perfectly ordinary verbs: answer, check, wash, drive, move, wait, cancel, explain, promise.

The Short-Term Bargain

Why does accommodation persist if it is so costly?

Because it often works in the short term.

Priya is distressed. Marcus runs the extra rinse. Priya's distress drops. Marcus's evening becomes quieter. Both people have just received a reason to repeat the same solution tomorrow.

This is not proof of a simple reinforcement mechanism in every couple, and it does not mean the person with OCD is calculating how to train a partner. Much of the pattern is desperate, automatic, and unwanted. But short-term relief can make a behavior very sticky.

The same bargain appears in reassurance. The answer settles the moment, so another answer seems reasonable when the doubt returns. It appears in avoidance. Canceling the restaurant ends the contamination crisis tonight, which makes canceling easier next time.

Family accommodation can therefore solve the immediate problem while making the household increasingly dependent on the solution.

Direct and Indirect Accommodation

Some accommodation is obvious because your partner asks for it.

"Check the door."

"Tell me that thought doesn't make me dangerous."

"Wash your hands again."

"Don't invite them."

Other accommodation happens without a request.

You stop mentioning a colleague because you know it starts a relationship-doubt loop. You silently clean a counter before your partner sees it. You pay for a taxi because the train is difficult. You move a knife to another room because intrusive thoughts are likely to start a reassurance spiral. You avoid a television program because the theme may lead to hours of questions.

These acts can be caring. Some may be practical choices you want to keep. The important point is that accommodation can become anticipatory. You begin organizing life around preventing distress before distress appears.

That is one reason the household can shrink without an obvious confrontation.

Do Not Pathologize Every Compromise

Couples accommodate each other constantly in the ordinary sense of the word.

One person dislikes strong smells, so the other opens a window. One works early, so the television stays low at night. One has a migraine, so plans change. One hates motorway driving, so the other usually drives. Relationships contain preference, disability, health needs, culture, habit, fairness, generosity, and negotiated inconvenience.

An OCD accommodation target needs more than "my partner wants this."

Look for the function. Is the behavior primarily serving a repetitive attempt to reduce obsessional distress or complete a compulsion? Is it becoming more elaborate? Does it transfer responsibility for uncertainty? Does it make ordinary life increasingly conditional on a ritual or avoidance rule?

If the answer is unclear, do not diagnose the behavior by force. Mark it as uncertain and bring it to an OCD-informed clinician if possible.

This matters especially with disability, chronic illness, pregnancy, trauma histories, religious practice, sensory needs, and real medical restrictions. A partner's legitimate access need is not an OCD symptom because it inconveniences you.

Accommodation Can Become Invisible

The strongest accommodations are not always the dramatic ones. They are often the arrangements nobody discusses anymore.

A certain chair is "hers."

A certain towel is "clean."

The children know not to touch the grocery bags.

You take the photos before leaving home.

You answer the moral question with the approved wording.

You handle online banking because a mistaken transfer feels intolerable.

You do not mention a past relationship.

Nobody calls these rituals. They are just how the household works.

To change them, you need an **OCD Footprint**, which Chapter 4 will build in detail. Before that, this chapter asks you to complete an Accommodation Map.

Build the Accommodation Map

Use a page with five columns. List behaviors you perform, not behaviors your partner performs.

What I do	Type	What usually comes before it	Short-term effect	Cost to ordinary life
Answer whether the door is locked	Reassurance	We are leaving home	We leave after several answers	Late, tense, responsible for certainty
Check the banking app for mistakes	Delegated checking	Transfer or bill	Anxiety drops briefly	I manage all shared banking
Ask visitors to wash twice	Routine modification	Someone comes over	Visit becomes possible	Guests avoid our home
Drive instead of taking the train	Facilitated avoidance	Travel	Trip happens	Routes and costs restricted
Repeat a phrase exactly	Participation	Intrusive moral doubt	Conversation ends for a while	I feel scripted

Do not use the word *cost* only to mean money. Cost can be time, flexibility, sleep, privacy, spontaneity, intimacy, social contact, parenting freedom, resentment, or responsibility.

For each line, ask one question: "If OCD-related distress were not driving this situation, would we still do it this way?"

A "yes" suggests it may be an ordinary preference or practical arrangement. A "no" makes it a stronger accommodation candidate. "I don't know" is a valid answer.

Rank by Changeability, Not Annoyance

The accommodation you hate most is not always the best place to start.

Suppose Marcus most resents that visitors cannot sit on one sofa. Removing that rule may provoke a large contamination crisis and affect Priya's sense of control over the home. Meanwhile, he also answers the same laundry question four times every evening. The repeated question may be easier to change first.

A good first **accommodation target** has three qualities.

It happens often enough that you can practice a new response.

It is low enough in genuine safety stakes that you are not experimenting with an emergency.

It is specific enough that both people can tell what is changing.

"Stop enabling OCD" is not a target.

"After I answer the locked-door question once, I will not answer it again during the same departure" is a target.

"Stop contamination rules" is not a target.

"I will use the kitchen sink without completing the extra rinse you ask me to do" is a target.

Precision reduces conflict because the limit is visible.

What If Your Partner Never Asked You to Do It

You may discover that some accommodations are yours.

You check the stove before Daniel asks because you cannot bear being late again. You cancel with friends before Priya can object because you are tired of the argument. You avoid telling Elena about a minor mistake because you know it will become a confession loop.

Those are especially useful first targets because you can change your own behavior without asking your partner to agree that they have OCD or to begin treatment.

You can simply stop pre-solving.

That may expose a request that had been hidden. If Daniel asks, "Why didn't you check the stove before I came downstairs?" the couple now has the real interaction in front of them. That can feel worse at first because the system is no longer running silently. Visibility is not the same as deterioration.

Accommodation and Anger

Partners often hesitate to reduce accommodation because they have seen what happens when a ritual is interrupted.

Clinical reviews note that attempts to reduce family accommodation can be associated with increased distress and, in some families, conflict or aggressive behavior. That possibility should be taken seriously without treating anger as inevitable. (Albert et al., 2017)

If your partner becomes disappointed, anxious, or argumentative when you change an accommodation, Chapter 9 will help you hold the limit without extending the debate.

If there are threats, intimidation, property destruction, physical violence, coercive control, or fear for a child or dependent person, this is no longer a simple accommodation problem. Safety planning and professional support take priority. Do not use a boundary exercise as a test of whether someone will become violent.

Keep Love Out of the Defendant's Chair

Accommodation often acquires a moral story.

"If you loved me, you would check."

"If I were a better partner, I could answer one more time."

"If I stop helping, I am abandoning them."

These stories make a behavioral change feel like a referendum on the relationship.

Try a different frame: love describes the relationship; accommodation describes a function.

You can love someone and check the stove. You can love someone and stop checking the stove. The question is which behavior you want to practice in a relationship affected by OCD.

That is why this book avoids the word *enabling* as its main label. *Enabling* can carry blame and imply intention. *Family accommodation* is more precise. It tells you what to observe.

In a Nutshell

Family accommodation is the participation of relatives or partners in OCD-related compulsions, reassurance, avoidance, delegated tasks, or routine changes. Research consistently finds that accommodation and OCD severity are related, while the direction of influence is not captured by correlation alone.

Your job is not to count all the ways you have failed. It is to make invisible patterns visible.

Complete the Accommodation Map. Choose one possible accommodation target based on frequency, safety, and specificity, not on which behavior makes you angriest.

In Chapter 3, you will learn the four-part response that gives you something to do in the exact moment a request arrives.

Chapter 3: Use the Support Pivot

Elena had learned to answer Jonah's work questions quickly.

"Do you think that email sounded aggressive?"

"No."

"Really?"

"Really."

"Even the last sentence?"

"No, the last sentence was fine."

That afternoon she tried something different. Jonah asked the same question for the third time. Elena did not open the email again.

"I think we're in the repeat loop," she said. "I know you're worried about how you came across. I gave you my view once, and I'm not going to keep checking the message. You can leave it sent, or you can use whatever plan you have for the doubt."

Jonah did not like the answer. But he knew what Elena was doing.

That structure is the Support Pivot.

The Four Moves

The Support Pivot gives you a response when the request arrives faster than your ability to think.

Notice the pattern. Identify what the request is doing.

Meet the person. Respond to distress, effort, or the relationship without certifying the feared conclusion.

Decline the accommodation. State what you will not do.

Return the next choice. Give responsibility back to your partner, or return together to ordinary life.

The sequence matters. If you begin with a refusal, your partner may hear only rejection. If you stop after empathy, you may slide into reassurance. If you decline accommodation but then decide what your partner must do next, you have replaced ritual participation with control.

The method is simple enough to remember because difficult moments do not reward complicated scripts.

Move One: Notice the Pattern

You do not have to announce this step aloud.

Jonah asks, "Can you read the email one more time?"

Elena asks herself: Is there new information? Has something actually changed? Is this a first request for feedback, or another attempt to obtain certainty?

Marcus hears, "Can you just wash your hands before you touch the remote?"

He asks: Is there an ordinary hygiene reason here, or is this part of the contamination rule we mapped?

Maya hears, "Promise you still love me after what I said."

She asks: Are we repairing a real conflict, or is this the fifth request for a guarantee after the conflict has already been discussed?

A strong pattern decision uses history without pretending to read your partner's mind. You do not need to know whether the question is "really OCD" at a metaphysical level. You need enough information to decide whether *you* will repeat the behavior you identified as an accommodation target.

When uncertain, use cautious language.

"This feels like the same question coming back."

"I think I'm being pulled into checking again."

"We may be in the certainty loop."

That is different from "OCD is making you do this." The first describes your observation. The second claims authority over your partner's internal state.

Move Two: Meet the Person

Meeting the person means answering the human fact that is obvious without answering the certainty demand.

"I can see you're scared about the email."

"I know leaving without another check feels rough."

"I get that this uncertainty is loud right now."

"I know you want an answer you can trust."

"That was a painful argument. I want to repair what actually happened."

These sentences can feel dangerously close to reassurance because they are kind. Kindness is not the problem. The question is whether the sentence certifies safety, morality, memory, health, love, or another feared conclusion in a repetitive loop.

"I know this is hard" is emotional acknowledgment.

"I know nothing bad will happen" is a prediction.

"You look frightened" describes what you can observe.

"You definitely didn't hurt anyone" supplies certainty.

You do not need to sound like a therapist. In fact, a relationship can become stranger when one partner starts speaking in clinical formulas. Use words you would normally use.

"Yeah, I know. This is awful."

"I can tell you really want me to check."

"I'm here. I'm just not doing that part."

Warmth can be plain.

Move Three: Decline the Accommodation

The decline should name your behavior.

"I won't check the lock again."

"I'm not going to answer the same question again."

"I won't ask the children to wash for a second time."

"I'm not reading the message again."

"I won't cancel the reservation because of this fear."

This is a **partner limit**, not an instruction.

Compare:

"You need to stop asking me for reassurance."

"I won't keep answering the reassurance question."

The first tries to control your partner. The second controls your participation.

Compare:

"You have to sit with the anxiety."

"I'm not doing the check. You can decide what you want to do next."

The first assigns treatment. The second returns choice.

A limit can still have consequences. If your partner continues asking the same question and you become overwhelmed, you may end the conversation for a period: "I'm going to make dinner. I won't keep discussing this question." You are not required to remain in an endless interaction to prove that your boundary is compassionate.

Move Four: Return the Next Choice

OCD often tries to move responsibility across the relationship.

"If you won't check, what am I supposed to do?"

The Support Pivot does not answer by prescribing a home exposure. It returns agency.

"If your therapist gave you a plan for this, this seems like a time to use it."

"You can decide whether to leave now or take a minute. I'm leaving the lock as it is."

"We can keep watching the film, or you can take some time. I'm not checking the symptom."

"I'll go with the ordinary plan we made."

"Do you want company while the urge passes, without talking about whether the fear is true?"

When there is no treatment plan, the next choice may simply be ordinary life. Put on shoes. Finish dinner. Go to bed. Return to the conversation you were having before the reassurance question arrived.

You do not have to create a therapeutic activity.

The One-Sentence Version

Some moments do not permit four sentences.

Use one sentence that contains warmth and a limit.

"I know you want certainty, and I'm not going to check again."

"I care that you're scared, but I won't repeat the answer."

"I want to stay with you, and I won't do the washing rule."

"I'll help with the practical problem once, not with repeated checking."

These are not magic phrases. If you repeat them fifteen times, they can become another form of reassurance. After one clear response, reduce language.

"Same answer."

"We talked about this."

"I'm not adding more certainty."

Then return to what you were doing.

The Support Pivot Is Not a Debate Technique

A frequent failure looks like this:

Partner: "Are you sure the door is locked?"

You: "I think that's reassurance seeking, so I won't answer."

Partner: "But I'm asking whether you actually locked it."

You: "Yes, but you always do this."

Partner: "So you didn't lock it?"

You: "I didn't say that. I said you're reassurance seeking."

Partner: "Why can't you answer one simple question?"

You: "Because reassurance maintains OCD."

Now you are debating whether the question qualifies as reassurance. The content changed, but the courtroom stayed open.

If you genuinely know you locked the door and this is the first practical question, you can answer once: "Yes, I locked it." If the question repeats, pivot. If you do not know whether you locked it, say that. Do not use OCD language to hide uncertainty you actually have.

The method works best when it is attached to a pre-agreed accommodation target. Surprise clinical labels during an argument are rarely persuasive.

Timing Changes the Meaning

A boundary announced while distress is at its peak can sound like punishment even when it is clinically sensible.

The International OCD Foundation's family guidance recommends discussing limits ahead of conflict when possible. NICE likewise says family involvement in compulsive behavior, avoidance, or reassurance seeking should be reduced sensitively and supportively. (National Institute for Health and Care Excellence, 2005; Van Noppen & Pato, 2009)

Use calm periods for the policy conversation.

"I've noticed I answer the same health question a lot. I think it gives us both short relief but keeps me in the loop. I want to change my part. From now on, I'll answer a normal first question if I actually have information. If the same certainty question comes back, I'll say I don't want to keep answering it."

That is clearer than inventing a rule during the fifth ask.

If your partner refuses the policy conversation, you can still set a limit on your behavior. Cooperation is preferable. Consent is required for treatment, not for your decision to stop performing a nonessential ritual.

Three Common Mistakes

The first mistake is **cold efficiency**.

"That's OCD. No."

It may be technically consistent but relationally expensive. If you can add one human sentence without feeding the loop, do it.

The second mistake is **the lecture**.

"I've been reading the research, and family accommodation is associated with symptom severity, so every time I reassure you I'm reinforcing the cycle."

That may be true as a general explanation, but it is poor timing when someone is already asking for certainty. Teach the concept outside the moment.

The third mistake is **covert reassurance**.

"I'm not going to reassure you, but if I thought you were actually dangerous, I would tell you."

For a person asking, "Am I dangerous?" that may function as reassurance in a lab coat.

The answer is not to become evasive about real safety. It is to stop smuggling the feared conclusion into every boundary sentence.

Practice Before the Hard Moment

Take one accommodation target from Chapter 2 and write three versions of your Support Pivot.

For a repeated checking request, you might write:

Full version: "I think this is the same checking loop. I know leaving feels uncertain. I already did the ordinary check, and I won't do another one. We can leave now, or you can take a minute and catch up."

Short version: "I know you want another check. I'm not doing one."

Repeat version: "Same limit."

For a contamination rule:

Full version: "I know this feels contaminated to you. I'm going to use the remote normally, and I won't wash again. You can decide whether you want to keep watching."

Short version: "I hear the concern. I'm not doing the extra wash."

Repeat version: "No change."

For relationship reassurance:

Full version: "I love you, and we already talked about what happened. I don't want to keep proving what it means about our whole relationship."

The first three words may be ordinary relationship care. If "I love you" itself is the repeated certainty target, choose a different opening: "I know this doubt is painful, and I'm not going to run the relationship test again."

When the Pivot Fails

Sometimes the request keeps coming. Sometimes your partner becomes angry. Sometimes you cave after ten minutes and answer.

That does not invalidate the method.

The Support Pivot is a practice for changing your behavior, not a device that makes your partner calm down on schedule.

If you answer after holding the limit for ten minutes, note what happened. Were you tired? Did you choose a target that was too difficult? Was the limit unclear? Did you keep debating after the refusal? Did the interaction contain a real issue that needed attention?

Then reset.

A lapse is information. It does not require a confession or a dramatic restart.

In a Nutshell

The Support Pivot is the book's main response tool: notice the pattern, meet the person, decline the accommodation, return the next choice.

It keeps two truths together. Your partner may be experiencing genuine distress, and you do not have to perform the certainty, checking, avoidance, or ritual function that distress is requesting from you.

Write the full, short, and repeat versions for one accommodation target. Practice saying them out loud when neither of you is upset. Plain speech is easier to use under pressure when your mouth has already formed the words.

Chapter 4 will widen the view from one request to the whole pattern of time, space, money, sleep, social life, and intimacy that OCD may be occupying.

Chapter 4: Find the OCD Footprint

Tessa first thought the problem was bedtime.

Amir's checking routine had stretched, and she was waiting forty minutes for him to come upstairs. When she mapped a week, bedtime turned out to be only one piece. She was also texting photographs of the unplugged iron before work, avoiding two streets on the drive home, moving packages into a "safe" area by the door, declining last-minute invitations, and answering health questions during lunch.

None of those acts was enormous. Together they formed a second schedule laid across their life.

The OCD Footprint is the amount of shared life organized around preventing, reducing, or resolving OCD-related distress.

You cannot change what you have not mapped.

Map Domains, Not Only Rituals

Most couples can name the obvious ritual. The more useful exercise is to ask where accommodation has changed a domain of life.

Time includes lateness, waiting, repeated conversations, checking before departure, washing sequences, bedtime delays, and time spent helping recover from a ritual.

Space includes rooms, furniture, surfaces, car seats, sides of the bed, routes, stores, bathrooms, and places that have become restricted or specially managed.

Work and money include missed shifts, interrupted calls, repeated checking of transactions, replacement purchases, taxis, extra cleaning supplies, medical consultations sought mainly for reassurance, and lost opportunities.

Sleep includes delayed bedtime, waking for questions, sleeping separately because of rituals, alarm routines, and repeated checks after lights out.

Social life includes visitors, restaurants, travel, family events, religious gatherings, children's activities, and friendships you have stopped arranging.

Intimacy includes touch rules, contamination fears, confession loops, relationship testing, sexual avoidance, and conversations that become repeated examinations of attraction or loyalty.

Parenting and family include rules children are asked to follow, questions children are asked to answer, relatives recruited into checking, and family plans changed around compulsions.

The footprint can be large even when symptoms are mostly invisible. Mental rituals may happen privately while the partner is recruited mainly for reassurance or avoidance.

Direct Cost and Indirect Cost

Direct costs are easy to count.

You spent twenty-two minutes checking.

You drove twelve extra miles.

You replaced food that was considered contaminated.

You canceled a ticket.

Indirect costs are quieter.

You stopped asking friends over.

You do not raise certain subjects.

You cannot leave the house spontaneously.

You sleep with one ear open for the next question.

You let your partner choose every route because arguing takes too much energy.

You no longer know whether you dislike something or have simply adapted to avoiding it.

Indirect cost matters because it tells you where **ordinary life** has been displaced. Ordinary life is the book's name for household, relationship, work, sleep, social, and personal activity chosen for its own value rather than organized around OCD.

The goal of accommodation reduction is not merely fewer rituals. It is more ordinary life.

Use a Seven-Day Footprint Scan

For one week, notice accommodations under six headings: time, space, money/work, sleep, social life, and intimacy/family.

Do not measure your partner's symptoms. Measure changes to your own behavior and shared routines.

Domain	Accommodation I noticed	Approximate cost	What ordinary choice was displaced
Time	Repeated review of a text message	25 minutes	We did not eat until late
Space	One chair treated as contaminated	Whole week	Nobody used the best reading chair

Domain	Accommodation I noticed	Approximate cost	What ordinary choice was displaced
Money/work	Took a taxi to avoid train	$38	Chose transport by fear rather than plan
Sleep	Answered health questions after midnight	35 minutes	Both stayed awake
Social	Canceled lunch with friends	One plan	Lost social time
Intimacy/family	Asked child to confirm a check	3 questions	Child became part of ritual

Approximate is enough. This is not an audit for prosecution.

Look for Rules With No Meeting Behind Them

A useful clue is the rule nobody remembers agreeing to.

"Packages go there."

"Nobody uses that towel."

"We don't eat at that restaurant."

"You handle the bills."

"We leave forty-five minutes early."

"Your sister can't bring her dog."

"We don't talk about your ex."

Some of these may be reasonable preferences. Ask how the rule got its authority.

Was it discussed as a shared choice? Is it flexible? Can either person propose changing it without a crisis? Does the rule primarily reduce OCD-related distress or uncertainty? Has it become more restrictive over time?

A household rule becomes clinically interesting when it is rigid, fear-driven, costly, and defended as necessary for certainty or ritual completion.

Do not use this test to win ordinary domestic arguments. "I prefer shoes off in the house" is not an OCD rule simply because you prefer shoes on.

Separate Preference From Compulsion

This distinction deserves care because partners can become overconfident once they learn the language of accommodation.

Suppose Grace wants food stored a particular way. It could be an OCD contamination rule. It could also be a cultural habit, a food-safety practice, a sensory preference, or simply how she likes the kitchen.

Ask four questions.

What feared outcome is the rule meant to prevent?

What happens if the rule is not followed?

How much certainty is required before the task feels complete?

Can the rule bend for context without a prolonged distress-and-ritual sequence?

The more the answer points toward feared consequences, repetitive neutralizing, escalating certainty, and inflexibility, the more likely you are dealing with an OCD-related process. If the answer is unclear, keep the label provisional.

The partner's job is not to become a home diagnostician.

Measure Your Behavior, Not Their Distress

Once people learn about family accommodation, they often start tracking whether refusing "worked."

"My partner was only anxious for ten minutes, so that was good."

"My partner was anxious all evening, so I must have done it wrong."

That measurement is unreliable. Distress can rise when a ritual is not completed. It can also rise for unrelated reasons. The purpose of a partner limit is not to make anxiety follow your preferred curve.

Track what you control.

Did you perform the check?

How many times did you answer?

Did you change the route?

Did you cancel the plan?

Did you ask the children to participate?

Did you stay in the debate?

This is the principle of **partner behavior before symptom outcome**. You may care deeply about your partner's distress while refusing to use it as the scoreboard for your own boundary.

Notice Accommodation Chains

One request can generate several accommodations.

Amir worries that a package is contaminated. Tessa moves it to a special area. Because it cannot touch the floor, she puts down paper. Because the paper may have touched the package, she throws it away with tongs. Because the bin is now questionable, she washes the handle.

The original request was "move the package." The footprint contains four additional behaviors.

Reassurance chains work similarly.

"Did I upset him?"

"No."

"How do you know?"

"Because he was laughing."

"Was he laughing before I spoke?"

"I think so."

"So you aren't sure?"

Now the partner is not answering one question. They are maintaining an evidence tree.

When you select an accommodation target, decide whether you are targeting the first behavior or the whole chain. Early in change, it is usually clearer to target the first behavior: "I won't move packages into the special area." That prevents the downstream sequence without requiring four separate refusals.

Find the Hidden Partner Adaptations

Some footprint items are not requested by your partner at all.

You stop wearing a certain perfume because it becomes a contamination discussion.

You check your own memory before mentioning an event because you anticipate moral reassurance questions.

You put important objects where they cannot be included in checking rituals.

You conceal minor health symptoms because you cannot face an evening of online research.

You schedule appointments around ritual time without saying why.

These adaptations matter because they show what OCD has taught *you* to do.

Pick one and ask, "What would I do here if I were not organizing around the expected reaction?"

That answer points toward ordinary life.

Choose a Restoration Target

An accommodation target names what you will reduce.

A **restoration target** names what you want back.

Accommodation target: stop doing the third lock check.

Restoration target: leave home within ten minutes of the planned time.

Accommodation target: stop asking visitors to follow the extra washing rule.

Restoration target: have two friends over for dinner.

Accommodation target: stop answering relationship certainty questions after bedtime.

Restoration target: sleep from midnight to seven without OCD conversations unless there is a real emergency.

Both targets matter. Reduction gives you a behavior to stop. Restoration gives the relationship a reason to change.

Without restoration, accommodation work can feel like a long list of refusals.

What If the Footprint Is Huge

A large map can produce urgency.

Do not respond by changing ten things.

A footprint took time to form. Some parts may be tied to treatment plans, disability, safety, finances, children, or long-running relationship conflict. Some accommodations may be much harder to change than others.

Use the map to sequence, not to attack.

Mark each item with one of four letters.

K means keep for now because it is ordinary, safety-related, unclear, or not worth the cost of changing.

L means low-difficulty candidate.

M means medium-difficulty candidate.

H means high-difficulty candidate that may need professional support or better planning.

Start with an L.

A graded plan can eventually reach larger parts of the footprint. A purge usually creates a bigger conflict than your skill set can hold.

When the Footprint Reveals a Relationship Problem

Sometimes mapping shows that not everything is OCD.

You may discover that money decisions are unequal even when no obsession is active. Your partner may use anger to control ordinary choices. You may have unresolved trust problems. You may disagree about cleanliness for reasons that predate OCD. You may be carrying most domestic work because of gender expectations rather than symptoms.

Do not force those problems into the accommodation frame.

OCD can coexist with unfairness, incompatibility, poor communication, abuse, depression, substance use, disability, or ordinary relationship strain. One diagnosis does not explain a whole person or a whole couple.

Later chapters will help you keep the categories separate.

Use the Footprint to Decide What Not to Change

A useful map also contains deliberate non-targets. Mark two accommodations you will leave alone this month.

One may be too entangled with safety to change without advice. Another may cost very little and matter greatly to your partner. A third may be an ordinary compromise you have consciously chosen.

Writing "not now" prevents the map from becoming an accusation that every adaptation is wrong.

For each non-target, write the reason.

"We are keeping the current medication organizer because it is a practical safety system, not a certainty ritual."

"I am not changing the sleeping arrangement this month because we are first protecting bedtime from reassurance conversations."

"I am keeping the shoes-off house preference because both of us want it."

This step strengthens the credibility of the targets you *do* choose. You are showing yourself that the aim is not to reverse every request your partner has ever made. The aim is to separate symptom-serving rules from the compromises and responsibilities you still endorse.

A good OCD Footprint therefore has three kinds of marks: reduce, clarify, and keep for now. That is a more mature map than a page covered only in red circles.

In a Nutshell

The OCD Footprint shows where accommodation has changed time, space, work and money, sleep, social life, intimacy, parenting, and family routines.

Map your behavior, not just your partner's rituals. Look for both direct costs and the ordinary choices that disappeared. Then pair one accommodation target with one restoration target.

The most important line on the map is not "what OCD made us stop."

It is "what we want to choose again."

Chapter 5 returns to the moment of reassurance and teaches you how to stop solving the content without becoming evasive or emotionally absent.

Part II: Change Your Side of the Loop

Chapter 5: Stop Solving the Content

Grace had answered the moral question six different ways.

Luis had told her about an intrusive thought from earlier in the day. He wanted to know whether having it meant he had secretly wanted something terrible to happen. Grace reminded him that thoughts are not intentions. He asked whether she was only saying that because she loved him. She explained again. He asked how she would know if he were actually a bad person. She gave examples from his behavior. He found exceptions to each one.

Grace eventually said, "I think we're trying to prove the thought harmless. I don't think more proof is going to finish this."

The conversation changed at that sentence because she stopped treating the fear as a case she could win.

Facts Rarely Settle a Certainty Problem

When someone you love is frightened by a question, facts are an obvious gift.

If the question is factual and answerable, facts help. The pharmacy closes at six. The form was submitted. The appointment is Tuesday. You did turn off the oven.

But an OCD reassurance loop often asks facts to perform a different task: abolish doubt.

The content can be health, contamination, morality, harm, religion, sexuality, mistakes, memory, or the relationship. The surface changes, yet the partner's role stays familiar. You become a researcher, witness, judge, scientist, theologian, doctor, detective, or mind reader.

That role expands because every piece of evidence contains uncertainty.

Suppose your partner asks whether a mole looks dangerous. You say it looks unchanged. They ask whether you remember its exact color. You compare a photograph. They question the lighting. You search the internet. A general warning introduces a new feature to inspect. By midnight, both of you know more about skin lesions and less about whether another answer will end the loop.

The issue is not ignorance. It is the use being made of information.

Use Process Language

Process not proof means naming what is happening between you instead of trying to settle the feared conclusion.

Proof language sounds like this:

"That can't happen because..."

"You definitely didn't..."

"Nobody would think..."

"I'm one hundred percent sure..."

"Here are the odds..."

Process language sounds like this:

"We've answered this once and the doubt is asking for a stronger answer."

"I think we're checking the same uncertainty from another angle."

"I don't have a new fact to add."

"This conversation is turning into a certainty test."

"We can deal with new information if it appears. I don't want to keep proving the current fear false."

Process language is especially useful when the content is impossible for you to know. You do not know how every person interpreted a conversation. You do not know that your partner will never get sick. You do not know exactly what a forgotten memory means. You do not know the future of a relationship.

You can be honest about that without sounding ominous.

"I can't promise what nobody can promise. I can decide what I'm doing with you today."

Do Not Turn Uncertainty Into a Slogan

Once partners learn that OCD treatment involves tolerating uncertainty, they can start saying "maybe, maybe not" to everything.

That can become mechanical and, in some couples, provocative.

Your job is not to perform an exposure script unless that is part of a clinician-guided plan you both accepted. You can simply decline the certainty task.

"I don't know, and I don't think we need to solve it again."

"I gave you the information I actually have."

"I don't want to speculate about that."

"We can respond if something real changes."

This is ordinary language. It keeps you out of the role of home therapist.

The First Answer Still Matters

A process-first approach does not mean withholding information.

Nia asks Owen, "Did you send the rent payment?"

"Yes. I sent it this morning."

That is an answer to a shared household question.

Ten minutes later: "Did you use the right account?"

"Yes."

Another ten minutes: "Can you show me the confirmation?"

Now Owen may recognize a checking pattern, especially if the couple has seen it before.

He can say, "I answered the payment question. I'm not opening the bank app to prove it again."

If Owen actually used a new account or is unsure whether payment went through, the facts have changed. He should check the practical issue once. The presence of OCD does not exempt either partner from real responsibilities.

The question is not whether information is forbidden. It is whether the interaction is still gathering information or has shifted into repeated certainty seeking.

Reassurance About Reassurance

A subtle loop appears when your partner asks whether *this* question counts as reassurance.

"Am I allowed to ask you whether the food is safe, or is that OCD?"

"What if I genuinely need to know?"

"How can I tell if I am asking normally?"

You may answer once by returning to the agreed framework.

"We said a first practical question is okay. Repeating it after an answer is the part we're reducing."

Then stop adjudicating each question in real time.

If you become the judge of whether every thought and question is OCD, the system has simply assigned you a new certainty job.

The same applies to treatment language. "Was that an exposure?" "Did I resist enough?" "Was my anxiety high enough?" If your partner is in treatment, those questions belong with their clinician or treatment plan, not with a partner who is being recruited to certify performance.

Health Questions Need a Two-Lane Response

Health-related OCD is difficult because real bodies create real uncertainty.

Use two lanes.

Practical health lane: new or materially changed symptoms, medication questions, test results, or medical advice that genuinely requires action. Use ordinary health care. Follow professional guidance. Do not let a book decide whether a symptom is medically important.

Reassurance lane: repeated inspection, repeated interpretation of the same stable information, repeated requests for probability estimates, repeated online searching done together, or repeated requests for you to certify that nothing is wrong.

The lanes can touch. A real symptom can trigger compulsive reassurance after appropriate care has already occurred.

A useful sentence is: "We followed the medical plan for this. I won't keep rechecking the same symptom tonight. If the situation changes in the way the clinician told us to watch for, we'll act."

Do not invent red-flag criteria yourself. Use the criteria a qualified professional has given, or seek appropriate medical advice.

Moral and Harm Questions Need the Same Discipline

Intrusive thoughts can involve subjects that are frightening precisely because they conflict with a person's values. OCD can attach to harm, taboo ideas, responsibility, religion, sexuality, or morality. NICE describes obsessions as unwanted intrusive thoughts, images, or urges and notes that such thoughts can be deeply distressing. (National Institute for Health and Care Excellence, 2005)

A partner can accidentally become a moral clearance office.

"Tell me I am not a bad person."

"Would a dangerous person worry this much?"

"Does the fact that I felt something mean I wanted it?"

"Promise I would never act on it."

If you repeatedly answer these questions, you may be participating in the certainty process even when your explanation is psychologically accurate.

You can meet the person without issuing a verdict.

"I know this thought is hitting something you care about."

"I hear how much certainty you want about what it means."

"I don't want to keep deciding your character for you."

If there is an actual threat, stated intent, plan, access to means, violence, or another real safety concern, do not assume it is OCD. Use the safety screen in Chapter 15 and appropriate professional or emergency support.

Relationship Facts Are Not Exempt

Relationship-centered questions are especially tempting to solve because you have direct information about your own feelings.

"Do you still love me?"

"Are you attracted to me?"

"Was that argument a sign we should break up?"

"Do you think we are compatible enough?"

Partners need to talk about these things. Chapter 12 will show how to separate genuine relationship work from repetitive tests.

For now, remember that a real answer can still be used compulsively.

You may say "I love you" because you want to say it. You do not have to say it twelve times in twelve formulations to make doubt disappear. When the repetition starts, the process becomes the target.

"I've answered you honestly. I don't want our relationship to become a test I have to keep passing."

That sentence protects intimacy better than pretending relationship questions are off-limits.

When Your Partner Argues the Evidence

A process response often produces a content counterattack.

"But you haven't considered the new detail."

"This time really is different."

"You misunderstood what I meant."

"You're refusing because you know I'm right."

The safest response is not necessarily silence. It is brevity.

"If there is genuinely new practical information, tell me once."

"I heard the detail. My response is the same."

"We can talk about the relationship issue tomorrow. I won't keep doing certainty checks tonight."

"I understand that you think this one is different. I'm still not repeating the review."

If you keep defending why you are not debating, you are debating.

Repair After You Get Pulled In

You will sometimes spend forty minutes proving a point before you realize what happened.

Do not turn that into a second forty-minute conversation about failure.

Say something like: "I think we got pulled into proving this. I'm stopping here."

If you were sharp or mocking, repair the sharpness.

"I was rude when I said that. I'm sorry. I still don't want to keep answering the question."

Repair does not require withdrawing the limit.

That distinction is important. Partners often collapse the two: either I hold my boundary and defend every word I said, or I apologize and give the reassurance after all.

You can apologize for delivery and keep the decision.

A Process-Not-Proof Worksheet

Take one reassurance topic that recurs. Write the content question at the top.

Then fill four lines.

What proof do I usually provide? List the evidence, explanations, searches, checks, or promises you give.

How does the question change after I answer? Note the next version.

What is the process? Repetition, probability seeking, moral certainty, memory checking, relationship testing, symptom inspection, or another pattern.

What process sentence will I use? One sentence only.

Example:

Content question: "Did I offend your sister?"

Proof I provide: replay the dinner, analyze tone, message sister, explain facial expression.

Question change: "But what about when she looked down?"

Process: repeated certainty about another person's internal state.

Process sentence: "I gave you my view once. I don't want to keep investigating what she might have thought."

Use the sentence this week. Do not judge success by whether your partner agrees with it.

Know When a Content Conversation Is Actually Needed

Process language should not become an escape hatch from real decisions.

If a doctor gives a new result, read the result. If a school sends a message about your child, discuss it. If your partner tells you that something you did hurt them, listen before deciding the conversation is reassurance. If a financial mistake has occurred, fix the mistake.

A practical test is whether the conversation can end with an action, decision, or repair that responds to current information.

"We need to call the bank" is actionable.

"We need to decide whether your memory proves you are a good person" is not.

"We need to apologize to your sister for what was actually said" is actionable.

"We need to establish with certainty what she secretly thought" is not.

This distinction prevents the phrase *process not proof* from becoming intellectual avoidance. You are not refusing facts. You are refusing to make facts carry an impossible burden after the ordinary problem has already been addressed.

In a Nutshell

OCD content can make you feel that one more fact will finally settle the matter. In reassurance loops, the standard of proof often moves as you meet it.

Use **process not proof**. Answer ordinary factual questions when you have ordinary factual information. When the same demand for certainty returns, stop litigating the fear and describe the repetitive process instead.

The goal is not to make your partner admit the question is OCD. The goal is to stop doing a job that no answer can finish.

Chapter 6 applies the same principle to delegated checking, where the task itself, not just the answer, has shifted onto you.

Chapter 6: Hand Back the Checking

Nia did not think of herself as checking for Owen.

She thought she was saving time.

Before bed, Owen asked whether the front door was locked. Nia checked it because she was closer. Then he asked whether she had pulled it firmly. She went back and tried the handle. Later he asked whether the oven was off. She looked. On the way out in the morning, he asked her to photograph the garage door.

The checks were now Nia's actions and Owen's relief.

When responsibility for a check moves from the person who feels the doubt to the partner, that is **delegated checking**.

Practical Checking and Compulsive Checking

Checking is part of ordinary adult life.

You confirm a child's car seat is fastened. You check the stove after cooking. You review a payment before sending it. You look for traffic before crossing a road. Shared households divide these responsibilities in all kinds of sensible ways.

A compulsive check differs by function and pattern. It is repeated beyond the ordinary task, seeks a level of certainty that the task cannot provide, or is performed to neutralize obsessional distress. OCD can involve overt checking as well as mental checking and reassurance seeking. (National Institute for Health and Care Excellence, 2005; Starcevic et al., 2012)

The partner problem begins when the request transfers the check, or the responsibility for whether the check was "good enough," onto you.

"Can you check it for me?"

"Can you watch me check so you can tell me I did it?"

"Can you take a picture?"

"Can you remember whether I touched it?"

"Can you check the account because I don't trust what I saw?"

One-and-done shared responsibilities can be perfectly ordinary. Delegation becomes an accommodation target when it is part of the same repetitive certainty process.

Responsibility Transfer Is the Hidden Cost

The visible cost of delegated checking is time.

The deeper cost is responsibility.

If Nia checks the oven, then Owen can ask whether *Nia* checked correctly. If she photographs it, the photograph becomes evidence to inspect. If she confirms he pulled the handle, her memory becomes the new object of doubt.

The uncertainty does not disappear. It changes owner.

That is why better checking technology rarely solves a certainty problem. A camera can be rechecked. A smart lock can display the wrong status. A photo can be unclear. A receipt can contain a mistake. A second person can remember incorrectly.

Technology is useful when it serves ordinary convenience or safety. It becomes accommodation when it is recruited to create impossible certainty.

Decide What Is Actually Your Job

Before reducing a delegated check, separate shared responsibility from ritual responsibility.

If you normally lock the house because you leave last, locking it once is your job.

If your partner normally cooks and asks you to inspect every burner after they have already checked, that second inspection may be accommodation.

If you manage shared banking by agreement, reviewing a payment before sending it may be your job.

If your partner asks you to reopen the banking app six times to prove a transfer did not go to the wrong account, that repeated review is different.

Write a one-sentence ordinary standard for the task.

"The person who leaves last locks the door once."

"The person who cooks turns off the stove and does one normal visual check."

"Shared payments are reviewed once before submission."

"Medication is taken according to the prescribed instructions and questions go to the pharmacist or prescriber."

An ordinary standard gives you something to return to. It prevents "stop checking" from becoming careless behavior.

Use the One-and-Done Principle Carefully

For many low-risk household tasks, **one-and-done** is a useful partner rule: complete the ordinary check once, then do not repeat it for certainty.

It is not a universal safety rule.

A pilot does not skip a required checklist because repetition feels compulsive. A clinician does not ignore medication verification. A parent may need to recheck a situation if new information changes the risk. A gas smell is a new fact. A warning light is a new fact. A child saying the buckle came loose is a new fact.

The principle applies to repetitive checking beyond the appropriate real-world procedure, not to professional or safety-critical standards.

When uncertain, follow the relevant professional or manufacturer guidance rather than a self-help shortcut.

Retire One Delegated Check

Choose one delegated check from your Accommodation Map.

For seven days, change only that task.

Nia might tell Owen: "I'm not going to photograph the garage door anymore. Whoever closes it will use the ordinary close-and-look check once."

Marcus might say to Priya: "I won't inspect your hands after you wash. I'm taking myself out of that check."

Elena might say to Jonah: "I won't reread sent emails to certify that nothing was wrong. If you want feedback before sending an important message, ask once before you send it."

The last example preserves a useful relationship function. Partners proofread for each other. The line is around repeated post-send checking for certainty.

Expect the Check to Shape-Shift

When one delegated check stops, the request may return in a different form.

"Fine, don't check the door. Just tell me whether you heard it click."

"I won't ask you to read the email. Can you tell me whether the subject line looked normal?"

"Don't inspect the stove. Just stand in the kitchen while I do."

This does not mean your partner is deliberately evading the rule. OCD is organized around uncertainty, and the next available route may feel genuinely different.

Use the function test.

Does the new request transfer responsibility, provide certification, or create another way to obtain certainty about the same feared outcome?

If yes, extend the limit.

"I don't think standing there changes the job. I'm not going to certify the check."

If the new request serves a different ordinary purpose, treat it on its own merits.

Digital Checking Can Consume a Relationship

Phones create endless evidence.

Read receipts, location sharing, bank alerts, door cameras, photographs, browser histories, health trackers, text screenshots, calendars, and smart-home logs can all become materials for checking.

Some couples use these tools because they are convenient or because they have agreed on practical safety reasons. The tool itself is not the problem.

Watch for repeated certification.

"Send me a photo so I know the stove is off."

"Share your location so I know you didn't take the dangerous road."

"Screenshot the message so I can check what I said."

"Open the health app so we can see the number again."

The partner can become an operator of a digital reassurance system.

If a device has a legitimate purpose, keep the purpose and reduce the ritual use. For example: "We keep location sharing for emergency and travel convenience. I won't answer repeated questions about the dot on the map."

Do not secretly change safety arrangements that affect both people. Discuss shared systems where possible.

What to Do With Distress Spikes

Suppose Owen usually asks Nia to check the stove. Tonight she declines. His distress rises sharply.

Nia may feel that she has created the distress and therefore must fix it.

She did change a familiar response. That can make the moment harder. It does not follow that repeating the check is the only kind option.

Use the Support Pivot.

"I know this is much harder without me checking. I'm not doing the stove check. I can stay here while you decide what to do next."

If Owen has a treatment plan, Nia can point him toward it without inventing an exposure.

If he does not, she can return to ordinary life. She does not need to supervise whether he checks for himself. Her target is her participation.

This distinction protects against a subtle role shift. A partner who stops checking can start monitoring whether the person with OCD is "responding correctly." That is still over-responsibility.

Refusing to Check Is Not Refusing All Help

Nia can refuse the garage-door photograph and still help carry groceries.

Marcus can refuse to inspect Priya's washed hands and still make dinner.

Jonah can decline to read an email for the fourth time and still help Elena prepare for a work presentation.

Keeping unrelated care in the relationship matters. Otherwise, accommodation reduction can become a global withdrawal that both people experience as punishment.

A useful sentence is: "I'm saying no to this check, not to helping you generally."

Then demonstrate it through normal partnership rather than repeating the sentence all night.

When the Check Is About You

Sometimes the partner is the object being checked.

"Did you wash your hands?"

"Did you look at anyone attractive?"

"Did you think that person was better looking than me?"

"Did you touch the package?"

"Did you tell me every detail?"

You may feel that because the question is about your own behavior, you owe a complete answer.

You owe honesty in the relationship. You do not owe endless certification.

Answer relevant practical questions once. If the same query repeats or demands impossible recall, name the process.

"I told you what I remember. I won't reconstruct it again."

"I answered the hand-washing question. I won't demonstrate it."

"We can talk about our agreement around fidelity. I won't submit to repeated attraction checks."

There may be genuine trust issues beneath some questions. Chapter 12 will show how to keep those issues available for real discussion without turning yourself into evidence.

A Checking Responsibility Card

Create one small table for the target you are retiring.

Question	Our ordinary standard
Who owns the task?	The person who performs it in ordinary life

Question	Our ordinary standard
What counts as complete?	One appropriate check
What counts as new information?	A material change, warning, or credible new fact
What will I stop doing?	Rechecking, photographing, certifying, or witnessing
What will I say?	"The ordinary check is done. I won't add another."

Keep the card for yourself. It is not a contract you wave during conflict.

The purpose is to decide before the request appears.

Practice an Ownership Handoff

Delegated checking often persists because both people have forgotten who owns the task.

Choose one recurring check and say the ownership sentence during a calm period.

"The person who cooks owns the normal stove check."

"You own deciding whether to send your work email. I can give ordinary feedback before you send it if I have time."

"I own locking the door when I leave last. I do not own proving it repeatedly afterward."

"Your medication questions belong with you and the prescriber. I can help with logistics, but I am not the dose checker."

An ownership sentence is different from "deal with it yourself." It specifies the ordinary responsibility and any help that remains.

If a task is genuinely shared, write the shared standard instead. "We review large transfers together once before sending."

The aim is not radical independence. Couples depend on each other. The aim is to remove the special layer in which one person's certainty becomes the other person's job.

In a Nutshell

Delegated checking transfers not only a task but also responsibility for uncertainty. The partner's check can become the next thing OCD questions.

Define the ordinary standard, then retire one nonessential delegated check for seven days. Keep real safety procedures intact. Respond to new facts when they are genuinely new. Refuse repeated certification.

Your job is to hand back the checking without becoming the checking police.

Chapter 7 moves from individual checks to the rules that can turn a shared home into an OCD-managed environment.

Chapter 7: Reclaim the Household

Simone noticed the couch rule when Caleb's brother sat in the wrong place.

Nobody shouted. Caleb simply froze, then asked Simone to get a sheet before his brother stood up. Simone had put down sheets hundreds of times. This time she heard the instruction as if it belonged to someone else's house.

The couch was not dangerous. The rule was there to make a contamination fear easier to live around.

By the end of the visit, Simone had a list: the couch, the guest towels, the grocery bags, the side door, the car seat, the "outside clothes," the package area, the kitchen sponge.

OCD had become an invisible landlord.

A Shared Home Needs Shared Rules

Home is where accommodation can become structural.

A reassurance question happens in conversation. A household rule can govern everyone before a word is spoken.

Do not touch that surface.

Use this bathroom, not that one.

Change clothes after coming inside.

Do not put groceries there.

Take a different route.

Do not invite that person.

Wash before sitting down.

Wait until the ritual is finished.

Family-accommodation research explicitly includes modifying routines and facilitating avoidance. The International OCD Foundation's family guidance also addresses preserving ordinary family routines and avoiding participation in compulsions. (Wu et al., 2016; Van Noppen & Pato, 2009)

The aim is not to make the home indifferent to the person with OCD. It is to return shared choices to shared decision-making.

Start With the Rule, Not the Fear

If the rule is "Nobody sits on the couch after using public transport," you can spend hours debating contamination.

How dirty are trains?

How long do germs live on fabric?

What counts as public transport?

Does a taxi count?

The rule will survive the debate because each answer creates another factual question.

Instead, name the household behavior.

"We have a rule that this couch is treated as contaminated after public transport. I don't want that to be a house rule anymore."

That statement is not claiming the couch is sterile. It is claiming that the shared home will not be organized around this standard.

A household limit is often clearer when it refers to what *people may ordinarily do* rather than what *OCD is forbidden to demand.*

"Guests can sit on the furniture."

"The children can use either bathroom."

"Groceries can go on the counter."

"We will leave for school at the planned time."

"We can invite family without requiring special washing."

These are restoration statements.

Preserve Legitimate Household Standards

Reclaiming the household is not a campaign against cleanliness, order, etiquette, or routine.

Homes need standards. People have preferences. Food safety matters. Illness can require precautions. Babies, older adults, allergies, immune conditions, pets, work uniforms, religious practices, and accessibility needs can all shape household behavior.

Use **ordinary standard plus flexibility**.

An ordinary standard can be explained without reference to preventing an obsessional catastrophe. It is proportionate to the task. It can adapt when circumstances change. It does not require repeated certification until it feels exactly right.

For example, washing hands before preparing food is an ordinary hygiene practice. Requiring every family member to wash in a particular sequence, for a particular duration, then avoid specific objects and receive inspection may be an OCD-related rule.

If the difference is uncertain, do not improvise a clinical ruling. Use professional guidance where medical risk is real.

Choose a Low-Risk Household Rule

Your first household target should not be the rule most central to severe symptoms.

Choose one with a visible restoration benefit and low genuine danger.

Simone chose the couch rule. She told Caleb beforehand: "I'm not going to put down a sheet for visitors anymore. They can sit normally. I know that may feel contaminated to you. I'm not asking you to like it, and I won't make guests follow the rule."

This was her part. She did not tell Caleb he had to sit on the couch himself.

That distinction matters. Reducing family accommodation is not the same as administering exposure. A partner can stop enforcing a rule on other people without forcing the person with OCD to perform a particular therapeutic task.

If Caleb is in ERP and his clinician has designed a related exposure with his consent, that plan may include more. Simone should follow the agreed treatment role, not invent one.

Restore One Ordinary Choice

Every household reduction should buy something.

If you stop the package ritual, what ordinary choice returns? Packages come inside and are opened where convenient.

If you stop the guest-washing rule, what returns? Friends can visit without being recruited into a ritual.

If you stop waiting for the checking sequence before dinner, what returns? The family eats at the agreed time.

Write the restored choice in plain language.

"We can use the living room without contamination zones."

"We can leave home when we are ready."

"The children can invite friends without special instructions."

"We can choose a restaurant for food and company, not for which surfaces feel safest."

The restoration target keeps accommodation work connected to life rather than to rule enforcement.

Visitors Should Not Become Participants

Accommodation often spreads to people who do not know what is happening.

A parent is told to repeat a phrase.

A friend is asked to wash again.

A babysitter is given a checking ritual.

A delivery driver is managed through elaborate contact rules.

A guest is asked to confirm what they touched.

You do not need to disclose your partner's diagnosis to everyone. Privacy matters.

You can set a household boundary without explanation.

"We don't need you to wash again."

"Please sit wherever you like."

"No need to answer that question again."

"We'll handle the door."

If your partner has chosen to tell someone about OCD, you can agree on language together. Avoid recruiting relatives into a coalition against the person with OCD. "We all know this is your OCD" can create shame and defensiveness.

Keep the target behavioral.

Children Need a Different Standard

Children should not be used as reassurance providers, checkers, contamination monitors, confessors, or ritual assistants.

If a child is already participating, remove responsibility in age-appropriate language.

"You do not have to answer that question again."

"Grown-ups will handle the door."

"You can use the chair normally."

"You don't have to check whether Mom washed."

Do not make the child responsible for challenging the parent's OCD. Do not ask the child to enforce a boundary that the adults cannot hold.

If symptoms are substantially affecting a child's safety, daily life, schooling, sleep, or emotional well-being, seek appropriate professional support. NICE specifically recommends assessing the impact of OCD-related rituals and compulsions on others, particularly dependent children. (National Institute for Health and Care Excellence, 2005)

Chapter 13 will return to this in depth.

When the House Becomes a Battleground

The danger in household change is that every ordinary action can become a statement.

You sit on the couch to prove a point.

Your partner cleans it to reverse the point.

You invite someone without warning because "this is my house too."

They cancel the visit.

Now the home is organized around resistance to OCD rather than accommodation of OCD. The disorder still controls the agenda.

Use advance notice where practical.

"This Saturday, my sister is coming over. I won't ask her to follow the extra washing rule. I wanted to tell you now so it isn't a surprise."

If the visit itself is a high-difficulty target, start smaller. Perhaps restore one chair, one room, or one routine first.

Graded change is not capitulation. It is sequence.

The Difference Between a Limit and a Trap

A limit says what you will do.

A trap engineers distress to force change.

"I will use the kitchen sink normally" is a limit.

"I rubbed the contaminated bag on your things so you'd learn" is a trap.

"I won't cancel my dinner because you are worried about contamination" is a limit.

"I invited ten people because exposure is good for you" is a trap.

Do not turn accommodation reduction into unauthorized exposure.

If you are angry about years of household restriction, the urge to force normality can feel righteous. It is still not your treatment role.

Reclaim your behavior and shared decisions without manufacturing fear.

Make a Household Agreement

A useful agreement is short enough to remember and specific enough to observe.

Include the rule being changed, the ordinary standard, what the partner will no longer do, and how the couple will handle distress or disagreement.

Example:

Rule being changed: Visitors must wash twice before sitting down.

Ordinary standard: Visitors follow normal hand hygiene and can sit where they choose.

My limit: I will not ask or signal visitors to wash a second time.

If distress rises: I will acknowledge that it is hard and keep the visit plan. I will not debate contamination.

Safety exception: If there is a real infectious-disease reason for precautions, we follow current medical or public-health guidance.

Keep one agreement for a week or two before adding another. Let the house experience the new rule enough times that it becomes less novel.

Respect Their Space Within Shared Space

A couple may decide that some personal areas remain under the person with OCD's control while shared areas use ordinary standards.

That can be a humane intermediate arrangement, not necessarily permanent.

For example, Caleb may keep a particular drawer organized in his preferred way while shared seating is no longer governed by contamination rules. Priya may handle her own laundry with whatever ritual she currently uses while Marcus stops following special rules for his clothes.

This approach separates *their compulsion* from *your participation.*

You are allowed to say, "I won't stop you from arranging your own shelf, and I won't arrange mine by the same rule."

Professional treatment may later address the person's own rituals. The partner does not have to do that work by force.

When Ordinary Preferences Clash

Once OCD has controlled a household for a long time, partners may discover they have genuine disagreements.

One likes a very clean kitchen. The other is relaxed.

One wants visitors often. The other needs quiet.

One wants shoes off. The other forgets.

Do not use the accommodation map to win every preference dispute.

Negotiate ordinary differences as ordinary differences. Compromise where you would compromise in a relationship without OCD.

The measure of success is not that the non-OCD partner gets their way. It is that choices are no longer made primarily to complete rituals or erase obsessional uncertainty.

Give Shared Space a Default

Households become exhausting when every object needs a custom ruling.

Choose a default for shared space: ordinary household use unless there is a specific, agreed reason for a different rule.

That means a new item does not automatically enter a contamination zone. A visitor does not automatically receive special instructions. A chair does not require a debate because someone wore outside clothes.

A default reduces decision fatigue. You can still make exceptions for real illness, allergies, repairs, cultural practice, or another shared reason.

Write the sentence privately first: "Shared space uses ordinary household rules unless we both agree on a specific exception."

Do not demand that your partner endorse the wording. Use it to guide *your* behavior.

If you discover that nearly every exception is unilateral and fear-driven, that tells you the household problem is larger than a single couch or sink.

In a Nutshell

A household can accommodate OCD through rules that outlive the conversation that created them.

Choose one low-risk rule. State the ordinary standard. Stop enforcing the OCD-related requirement on yourself or others. Pair the change with a restoration target so the household gains something concrete.

Do not manufacture exposures, recruit visitors as therapy tools, or turn children into boundary enforcers.

Chapter 8 will show how to sequence several accommodation targets without overwhelming the relationship.

Chapter 8: Change One Thing at a Time

Maya had a list of twenty-three accommodations by the time she finished the OCD Footprint.

She wanted to stop all of them.

Daniel wanted to stop none of them.

The compromise was not "eleven and a half." They chose one: Maya would no longer return to the apartment to check the stove after they had already left.

For two weeks, that was the whole plan.

The first few departures were hard. Then the new response became recognizable. The couple learned something more useful than whether Daniel's anxiety fell quickly: Maya could hold one clear limit without turning every request into a fight.

That is the logic of **graded reduction**.

Why Abrupt Withdrawal Is Usually a Poor Home Strategy

Once a partner learns that accommodation is clinically relevant, urgency is understandable.

You may think, "If this is part of the problem, I should stop immediately."

But a relationship is not a laboratory reset. Accommodation may be woven into transportation, meals, finances, children, sleep, access needs, and treatment. Sudden withdrawal can create confusion about what is changing and why. It can also make it impossible to tell which limits you can actually sustain.

Clinical guidance recommends reducing family involvement in compulsions, avoidance, and reassurance seeking sensitively and supportively. A small randomized trial of a brief family intervention showed that focused accommodation work can be useful alongside individual ERP, but the intervention was structured and the study was preliminary. (National Institute for Health and Care Excellence, 2005; Thompson-Hollands et al., 2015)

Your home plan should borrow the principle of structure, not pretend to reproduce a clinical protocol.

Build an Accommodation Ladder

Take the items marked L, M, and H on your OCD Footprint.

Rank them by difficulty *for you to change*, not by how "severe" your partner's OCD seems.

Low difficulty might include not rereading a routine text, not taking a second photograph, or not answering the same low-stakes question after bedtime.

Medium difficulty might include using a shared room normally, declining a regular avoidance route, or letting a visitor ignore a ritual rule.

High difficulty might involve children, sex, substantial money, housing, intense contamination restrictions, treatment-related conflict, credible anger, or routines that have controlled the home for years.

A ladder is not a diagnosis. It is a sequencing tool.

Level	Accommodation	Why this level	Restoration target
L	Stop second answer about locked door	Frequent, low real-world risk	Leave on time
L	Stop rereading sent casual messages	Clear repetition	Evenings without email review
M	Use shared couch normally	Visible household rule	Host friends
M	Take normal route to work	Avoidance has grown	Flexible travel
H	Change child-involved contamination rules	Affects dependent person, high conflict	Child free from ritual role

If an item has genuine safety ambiguity, do not place it on the ladder until that ambiguity is resolved.

Use One Behavioral Sentence

Each target needs a definition that can survive a bad day.

Weak target: "Give less reassurance."

Strong target: "After I answer an ordinary first question once, I will not answer the same certainty question again for the rest of that episode."

Weak target: "Stop checking."

Strong target: "I will no longer photograph the stove after the ordinary departure check."

Weak target: "Be less controlled by OCD."

Strong target: "I will attend my Thursday class even if my partner asks me to stay home because of a contamination fear."

Behavioral sentences reduce two problems. First, they limit overreach. Second, they prevent you from moving the goalposts when you are frustrated.

Tell Your Partner Before the Next Request

Whenever possible, announce the change during a calm period.

Use three parts.

What you noticed: "I've been answering the same door question several times each morning."

What you are changing: "I'll answer once if there's a normal practical question. I won't repeat the answer after that."

What remains: "I'm still leaving with you, and I'm happy to talk about how the morning plan is working when we're not in the middle of the question."

You do not need your partner to agree with the theory of family accommodation before you change your behavior.

You do need to avoid false consent. Do not say, "We agreed" if they did not. Say, "This is the limit I am setting on what I will do."

If the change affects shared finances, children, housing, medical care, or another mutual responsibility, unilateral action may not be appropriate. Separate your right not to perform a ritual from shared decisions that require discussion.

Keep the Target Stable Long Enough to Learn

Changing the rule every day creates more uncertainty for both people.

Suppose Maya refuses the stove check Monday, does it Tuesday because Daniel is tired, refuses Wednesday, then does three checks Thursday because they have guests.

Daniel cannot tell whether the limit is real. Maya cannot tell whether her script works because she keeps renegotiating it under pressure.

Consistency does not mean rigidity. Real safety information overrides a plan. A family emergency overrides a worksheet. A treatment clinician may recommend a different approach.

Within ordinary conditions, give one target enough repetitions to become recognizable.

A useful review period is one or two weeks, not because research has established that exact interval, but because it is long enough for multiple attempts and short enough to revisit deliberately.

Track Partner Behavior

Your tracking sheet should contain only variables you control.

Date	Target occurred	I accommodated	I used my script	I debated after the limit	Ordinary life restored
Mon	Yes	No	Yes	12 min	Left on time
Tue	Yes	Yes	No	0	Left late
Wed	Yes	No	Yes	2 min	Left on time
Thu	No	N/A	N/A	N/A	Normal morning

Do not add "partner anxiety score" unless a clinician has specifically asked for it as part of treatment.

The person with OCD is not your experiment.

You can note contextual facts if they help your own plan: "I gave in after sleeping four hours." That may tell you to choose a simpler script when exhausted.

Expect an Extinction Story, Not a Guaranteed Extinction Burst

Popular self-help language sometimes claims that behavior always gets worse before it gets better when reinforcement stops.

Do not turn that into a promise.

Your partner may ask more intensely after you change an accommodation. They may ask less. They may become quiet, angry, sad, inventive, relieved, or indifferent. The response depends on the person, the symptom, the relationship, and the context.

The useful point is simpler: short-term distress does not by itself prove the limit was wrong.

At the same time, increasing aggression, threats, coercion, or safety concerns are not a therapeutic milestone to endure. Chapter 15 separates discomfort from danger.

What Counts as a Successful Week

A successful week is not one in which your partner's OCD improves on schedule.

It is one in which you learned something reliable about your own behavior.

Perhaps you discovered that the first question is easy to answer once, but you get trapped when you explain why the second answer is unhelpful.

Perhaps your target was too broad.

Perhaps you can hold the limit at home but abandon it around other people because you feel embarrassed.

Perhaps the behavior stopped affecting the evening even though your partner still disliked the limit.

These are useful findings.

You are building a **partner limit** that can survive ordinary life.

When to Move Up the Ladder

Move to a second target when the first one is clear enough that you no longer have to invent your response each time.

That does not mean your partner never asks.

It means you know what you will do.

Add only one new target at first. Keep the old one in maintenance.

If both collapse, reduce the load rather than escalating your resolve through anger.

Graded reduction is not about being timid. It is about preserving learning.

When to Step Back

Step back and reassess if the target involves safety ambiguity, the plan is causing severe relationship conflict you cannot contain, you are acting as an unauthorized therapist, or the change affects a dependent person in ways you did not anticipate.

Step back also if you discover that the behavior is not an accommodation after all.

For example, you may stop a "checking ritual" and then learn that your partner's occupational role legally requires a documented double check. Restore the appropriate procedure.

Being willing to correct your own interpretation makes your limits more credible.

Do Not Stack Punishments Onto the Limit

A common escalation is:

"I won't reassure you, and if you ask again I'm leaving."

Sometimes leaving a repetitive conversation is a reasonable limit. But if every request accumulates a new consequence, accommodation reduction becomes a disciplinary system.

Use the smallest effective boundary.

"I won't answer the question again."

If the repetition makes it impossible to continue dinner: "I'm going to take twenty minutes in the other room. We can talk about something else afterward."

The second action protects your participation. It is not meant to make your partner regret asking.

Create a Four-Week Reduction Plan

Your first month can be modest.

Week 1: Observe and hold Target A.

Week 2: Continue Target A. Repair your script. Identify where you debate.

Week 3: Keep Target A and add Target B if the first response is stable.

Week 4: Review both targets and choose one restoration action that is bigger than the boundary itself.

A restoration action might be arriving on time to a weekly plan, having a visitor, going to your own class, using a shared room normally, or ending reassurance conversations before bedtime.

The full planning grid appears in Appendix C.

If Your Partner Is in ERP

Exposure and response prevention is a core evidence-based psychological treatment for OCD. NICE recommends CBT including ERP for adults with OCD at different levels of impairment and notes that involving a family member as a co-therapist may be considered when appropriate and acceptable. (National Institute for Health and Care Excellence, 2005)

"May be considered" is not "the partner should invent exposures."

Ask what role, if any, the clinician wants you to play.

Useful questions include: Which accommodations are we targeting? What exact response should I use? What should I do if distress rises? Are there safety exceptions? How will we know whether I am overstepping?

If you are not invited into treatment, keep your work on your side of the line: your reassurance, your checking, your routines, your time, your boundaries.

Keep a Waiting List, Not an Emergency List

Once you can see many accommodations, every one can feel urgent.

Create a waiting list with the next three possible targets and leave them there.

Do not work on them this week.

The list reassures *you* that noticing a problem does not require immediate action. It also helps prevent resentment from selecting the next target during an argument.

At the review date, choose from the waiting list using the same criteria: safety, specificity, frequency, and restoration value.

If a new issue appears before then, add it to the list unless it involves real safety or a dependent person.

A planned queue turns accommodation reduction from a reaction into a household practice. You stop lunging at whatever annoyed you most that day.

In a Nutshell

Change one accommodation target at a time. Define it behaviorally. Announce it in advance when possible. Track what *you* do. Keep the target stable long enough to learn.

Do not use your partner's distress as a pass/fail score, and do not treat escalation as proof that a boundary must be endured regardless of safety.

The next difficulty is predictable: what happens when your partner is angry, pleading, or convinced that your new limit is cruel.

Chapter 9 is about holding the line without turning the relationship into a courtroom.

Chapter 9: Hold the Limit Without a Fight

Marcus knew what he planned to say.

Priya asked whether he had washed after touching the delivery bag. He answered the first time. When she asked again, he said, "I already answered. I'm not going to keep reassuring."

Priya stared at him. "So now I'm not allowed to ask you questions?"

Marcus heard accusation and answered accusation.

"That's not what I said. You know that's not what I said."

"Then answer me."

"I did."

"If it was no big deal, you'd just answer."

Within thirty seconds, the conversation was no longer about hand washing. It was about whether Marcus was cruel, whether Priya was controlling, and which of them had ruined the evening.

A limit can be clinically sensible and still be delivered into a relationship with history, exhaustion, and fear.

Distress Is Not a Verdict

When accommodation changes, the person with OCD may feel more distress in the short term. That is not surprising. The old response was partly valuable because it reduced distress or made a feared situation easier to avoid.

It can be tempting to read the emotional reaction as evidence.

"They're crying, so I'm being cruel."

"They're angry, so the boundary is wrong."

"They're calm, so I did it perfectly."

None of those conclusions follows automatically.

Emotion tells you that something matters. It does not by itself tell you whether a partner limit is fair, whether a fear is true, or whether a clinical strategy is appropriate.

At the same time, do not turn this principle into license to ignore your partner. "Your distress doesn't prove anything" is not a sentence most relationships need.

Use it internally. Then respond to the person.

"I know you hate this change."

"I can see you're upset."

"I don't want to fight with you."

And keep the limit.

Validation Without Certainty

The word *validation* can become vague. In this book, it means recognizing an observable experience without confirming the feared conclusion.

You can acknowledge:

the distress,

the effort required,

the inconvenience,

the disappointment,

the frustration with you,

the fact that a new boundary is hard,

the relationship issue underneath the loop.

You do not have to confirm:

that the feared contamination happened,

that danger is zero,

that a thought has a harmless meaning,

that a relationship is guaranteed,

that your memory is perfect,

that the compulsion is necessary.

Compare these responses.

"I know it feels contaminated, and I won't do the extra wash."

"You are right, it probably is contaminated, but I won't wash."

The first meets the experience. The second certifies the content.

"I hear that you think I'm being unfair. I still won't check the door again."

"You are right, I am being unfair, but my book says I should do this."

The first leaves room for disagreement. The second turns the limit into self-punishment and invites another debate.

Do Not Defend the Boundary Forever

A partner limit becomes weaker when you explain it for twenty minutes.

Your partner says, "Why won't you answer?"

You say, "Because repeated reassurance seems to be part of the OCD loop."

They say, "But this is different."

You say, "I know it feels different, but we've answered the same question."

They say, "You can't know what OCD is."

You say, "I read that reassurance maintains symptoms."

Now you are litigating your right not to litigate.

Explain the limit once outside the heat of the moment. During the request, use the short version.

"I answered once."

"I'm not doing another check."

"I'm not asking the children to do that."

"I won't keep discussing whether the fear is true."

If the argument shifts to the boundary itself, schedule that conversation for later.

"We can talk tomorrow about whether this limit is working. I won't debate it while we're in the reassurance loop."

That protects the relationship from making every OCD moment into a policy meeting.

The Broken-Record Response

A **broken-record response** is one short sentence repeated without adding new reasons.

"I won't check again."

"But why?"

"I won't check again."

"You're not listening."

"I hear you. I won't check again."

"What if this time is real?"

"I won't check again."

Use this sparingly. Repeating the exact phrase twenty times can sound robotic and may become part of the ritual. After one or two repetitions, disengage from the topic if you can.

"I'm going to finish dinner. We can talk about something else."

The goal is not to win by endurance. It is to stop generating new material for the loop.

Anger Deserves Categories

Not all anger is the same.

A partner may be irritated: "This is ridiculous."

They may be distressed and loud: "Why are you doing this to me?"

They may insult you.

They may block a doorway.

They may threaten to harm themselves if you do not comply.

They may throw something.

They may threaten you, a child, a pet, or property.

Do not collapse these into "OCD backlash."

Clinical literature notes that family attempts to reduce accommodation can be associated with conflict and, in some cases, aggressive behavior. (Albert et al., 2017) That does not make aggression a normal exposure to tolerate.

Your response should match the category.

Irritation may call for a calm limit.

A heated argument may call for time apart and later repair.

Repeated insults may call for a relationship boundary.

Threats, coercive control, violence, or credible safety concerns call for safety planning and professional help. If there is immediate danger, contact appropriate emergency services.

Chapter 15 gives a fuller safety screen.

Do Not Bargain With Threats

Suppose your partner says, "If you leave without checking, I swear I'll smash the car window."

This is not a moment to prove that accommodation reduction works.

Prioritize safety. Leave if safe to do so. Get support. Use emergency services where appropriate. Do not remain in danger because you fear that responding to a threat will "reinforce OCD."

Behavioral principles do not cancel basic safety.

The same is true for threats of self-harm. Take credible threats seriously and seek appropriate professional or emergency support. You are not responsible for conducting a suicide-risk assessment at home.

A partner limit can be revisited later with professional help.

Guilt Can Pull You Back Into the Loop

Many partners experience guilt before the other person says anything.

You may think:

"They didn't ask to have OCD."

"I'm the one who read this book, so I am creating the change."

"They had a terrible day."

"It would take me ten seconds to check."

All of those statements may be true.

A ten-second check may also be the exact behavior you decided to change.

Use **compassion without reversal**.

"I know today was awful. I'm still not doing the second check. I can make tea and sit with you."

Notice the alternative care. You are not required to choose between ritual assistance and abandonment.

Resentment Can Make the Limit Too Big

Guilt pulls one way. Resentment pulls the other.

After years of accommodation, a partner may decide that the new boundary should compensate for all the old ones.

"No more questions about anything."

"I'm done changing a single plan for you."

"You can deal with your OCD yourself."

That is not graded reduction. It is a relationship verdict delivered through a clinical concept.

Some partners may legitimately decide that the relationship cannot continue as it is. Some may end relationships. Those decisions deserve direct discussion based on safety, compatibility, respect, and capacity.

Do not smuggle a breakup-level decision into a reassurance rule.

Say what the real issue is.

"I can no longer live with the current level of household restriction. We need a bigger conversation about what has to change for me to stay."

That is clearer than arguing over whether the light switch was checked.

Use a Repair Window

If a boundary interaction becomes ugly, do not force repair while the reassurance question is still active.

Set a **repair window**.

"That went badly. I want to talk about how we spoke to each other at seven tomorrow. I'm not going back to the contamination question tonight."

The repair conversation has a narrow agenda.

What did I say that I want to own?

What did you say or do that affected me?

Was the target clear?

Did I accidentally debate or shame?

Do we need to change the timing or wording?

Does the boundary itself still stand?

This keeps relationship repair separate from reassurance.

For example: "I called you irrational. That was disrespectful, and I'm sorry. I still won't inspect your hands after washing."

An apology that leaves the behavioral limit intact is not contradictory. It is mature.

When Your Partner Calls the Boundary Cruel

Do not immediately prove that you are kind.

Ask what they mean.

"What part felt cruel?"

They may say the tone was mocking. That is actionable.

They may say you walked away without explaining the new rule. That may be worth correcting.

They may say any refusal to reassure is cruel. You can disagree.

"I understand that not answering feels rejecting. I don't want to reject you. I also don't want to keep doing the repeated certainty answer."

If the conversation returns to whether the fear is actually true, stop.

"We can discuss how I set the limit. I won't reopen the content."

That sentence protects both accountability and the boundary.

Build an Exit Script

Some reassurance loops need a clean end.

Choose a script that fits your relationship.

"I've answered once. I'm done with this topic tonight."

"I'm going to the other room for twenty minutes. I won't discuss the checking question when I come back."

"We can talk about anything else. If the same question continues, I'm going to end the conversation."

"I need sleep. Unless there is a real emergency, I'm not doing OCD conversations after midnight."

An exit script should tell the person what *you* will do. Avoid threats about what they must do.

If the person follows you from room to room, blocks your exit, takes your phone, or prevents you from disengaging, that is a safety and coercion issue, not a communication exercise.

Score the Interaction on Three Things

After a difficult moment, score yourself on only three questions.

Did I keep the target clear?

Did I avoid unnecessary cruelty?

Did I return to ordinary life when possible?

You do not need to score how upset your partner was.

You do not need to score how calm you looked.

You do not need to score whether the conversation felt "therapeutic."

A sustainable partner limit can be imperfectly delivered and later repaired.

Learn the Difference Between Silence and Disengagement

After a limit, going silent can feel punitive if your partner does not know what is happening.

Disengagement is clearer.

"I am not discussing this question further. I can talk about dinner, tomorrow's plan, or something else."

You remain relationally available while closing one topic.

If you need physical space, name the time frame when it is safe to do so.

"I need twenty minutes. I will come back at eight."

You are not promising that the argument will be resolved at eight. You are promising that the pause is not a disappearance.

This distinction matters in relationships where withdrawal has its own history. Accommodation reduction should not accidentally recreate old patterns of stonewalling.

A good exit ends the loop and leaves a door open to ordinary contact.

In a Nutshell

A boundary is not proven wrong by distress, and it is not proven right by distress either.

Meet the person without certifying the fear. Keep explanations short. Separate the policy conversation from the live reassurance loop. Repair rude delivery without reversing a sound limit.

Treat threats, coercion, violence, and credible self-harm concerns as safety issues. Do not use accommodation reduction as a reason to remain in danger.

You have now learned the core behavior-change skills. Part III moves to the relationship roles around them, beginning with the line between being involved in treatment and becoming the therapist.

Part III: Stay a Partner

Chapter 10: Be a Partner, Not the Therapist

Elena knew enough about ERP to become dangerous to the relationship.

Jonah's therapist had explained exposure and response prevention. Elena understood the basic idea: face a feared situation or thought and resist the usual compulsion. Soon she was suggesting exposures at home.

"You should send the email without rereading."

"You should touch that and not wash."

"This is a perfect chance to practice."

Jonah began to hear clinical coaching in every disagreement. Elena began to treat his willingness to follow her suggestions as evidence of whether he was trying hard enough.

Both of them had crossed a line.

A partner can be part of treatment. A partner is not automatically the treatment provider.

Know the Treatment Basics Without Taking the Job

CBT that includes exposure and response prevention is a central evidence-based psychological treatment for OCD. ERP usually involves planned contact with feared thoughts, images, situations, or triggers while reducing rituals or neutralizing responses. Treatment is individualized, and medication, usually an SSRI, may also be part of care depending on the person's situation. (National Institute for Health and Care Excellence, 2005; NHS, 2023)

Knowing that much helps a partner understand why reducing accommodation can make sense.

It does not qualify a partner to design an exposure hierarchy, decide medication, assess risk, diagnose a symptom theme, or determine whether a difficult activity is therapeutically appropriate.

The **treatment role** is the limited, consent-based way a partner participates in professional OCD treatment.

The word *limited* matters.

Family Involvement Can Be Useful

NICE says that for adults with OCD who live with family or carers, involving a family member as a co-therapist in ERP may be considered when appropriate and acceptable. Couple-based approaches have also been developed to address accommodation and relationship processes while supporting ERP. (Abramowitz et al., 2013; National Institute for Health and Care Excellence, 2005)

That supports thoughtful family involvement.

It does not mean every partner should be a co-therapist.

The 2013 couple-based article described a treatment program and case material. It is not evidence that informal couple therapy, without OCD treatment, should replace established OCD care. NICE specifically notes that marital or couple therapy has not been shown to have a clinically important effect as a specific treatment for OCD. A couple may still use relationship therapy for relationship problems; that is a different claim. (Abramowitz et al., 2013; National Institute for Health and Care Excellence, 2005)

The cleanest rule is: if a clinician wants you involved, get the role in plain language.

Five Questions for a Partner Session

If your partner invites you to a treatment session, ask questions that define your job.

Which accommodations should I reduce first?

What exactly should I say or do when the request happens?

What should I avoid doing even if it feels helpful?

What counts as a real safety exception for this target?

How should we handle a lapse or a sharp increase in distress?

You may also ask how much treatment discussion should happen at home. Some couples benefit from a brief scheduled check-in. Others find that OCD takes over the relationship when treatment becomes a constant topic.

The clinician may give guidance specific to the person's symptoms. That guidance outranks a generic script in this book.

Consent Has Two Directions

Your partner has to consent to you being involved in their treatment information.

You also get to consent to the role being asked of you.

A clinician may suggest that you attend a session, help with a planned exposure, or change a specific accommodation. You can say yes, no, or ask for a smaller role.

"I can stop doing the door check. I don't want to run exposure exercises."

"I can attend one session. I don't want access to every detail of therapy."

"I can use the agreed reassurance response. I cannot monitor homework all day."

Being a supportive partner does not require becoming unpaid clinical staff.

If you already feel consumed by OCD, a very large treatment role may worsen that problem.

Do Not Become the Homework Police

Treatment homework can create a seductive new system.

"Did you do the exposure?"

"How anxious were you?"

"Did you ritualize afterward?"

"Are you sure you didn't mentally reassure yourself?"

The partner who used to certify safety is now certifying treatment performance.

Unless the clinician has specifically asked you to track something and your partner agrees, let treatment homework belong to the person in treatment.

You can ask relational questions.

"Do you want encouragement or space?"

"Is there something your therapist asked me to change?"

"Do you want me to come to the next session?"

That is different from supervising compliance.

Do Not Diagnose Every Disagreement

Once a couple learns OCD language, it can swallow ordinary conflict.

"I want us to leave earlier."

"That's your OCD."

"I don't like how you spoke to me."

"You're reassurance seeking."

"I don't want your parents staying for a week."

"That's avoidance."

Clinical labels can become weapons because they end discussion by placing one person's preference on the symptom side of the table.

Keep a separate lane for relationship problems.

If Grace says Luis's repeated questions are exhausting, that may be accommodation-related.

If Luis says Grace spends shared money without discussion, that is a financial relationship issue even if he also has checking compulsions.

If Priya wants the kitchen cleaner than Marcus does, they may have a preference conflict in addition to contamination OCD.

A diagnosis explains some behavior. It does not grant either partner interpretive sovereignty.

Medication Is Not Your Domain

OCD medication questions can become a form of accommodation too.

"Do you think this dose is enough?"

"Should I stop because I feel strange?"

"Are these side effects dangerous?"

A partner can help write down concerns, attend an appointment with consent, pick up a prescription, or notice changes they genuinely observe.

Do not give dosing instructions or advise stopping medication. NHS guidance warns not to stop an SSRI abruptly without speaking to a doctor, and medication decisions need professional oversight. (NHS, 2023)

Use a treatment-role sentence.

"That is a prescriber question. I can help you write it down or call the clinic."

If the situation appears medically urgent, seek appropriate medical care rather than waiting for a routine appointment.

Privacy Still Belongs in the Relationship

Treatment can expose intimate material. OCD obsessions may involve sex, religion, harm, morality, relationships, or taboo content.

Your partner does not have to tell you every intrusive thought in order for you to reduce accommodation.

You may need to know the *pattern*.

"For this symptom, I may ask you to reassure me that I am a good person. Please use the agreed response."

That can be enough.

You do not need a full confession to enforce your side of a reassurance limit. In fact, repeated confessional detail can itself become part of a compulsion in some presentations.

Respect privacy unless a real safety issue changes the equation.

When the Therapist's Plan Is Unclear

Sometimes a partner comes home with an instruction you do not understand.

"My therapist says you have to stop all reassurance."

"My therapist says you should make me do this exposure."

"My therapist says you are the reason I am not improving."

Do not argue about what the clinician "must have meant."

Ask for clarification with your partner's consent.

"I want to follow the plan accurately. Can we write down the exact partner instruction or ask together at the next session?"

If direct contact is not possible, stay with your own clear limits and avoid inventing treatment.

No competent clinical plan requires you to tolerate abuse or ignore real danger.

If Treatment Is Poorly Matched

Not every therapist has specialist OCD training. People with OCD can spend years in treatment that does not directly address compulsions, or they may have had experiences that make them skeptical.

A partner can suggest asking specific questions.

"Does this clinician regularly treat OCD?"

"Do they use CBT with ERP when appropriate?"

"How do they address reassurance and family accommodation?"

"Can they explain the treatment plan in plain language?"

The International OCD Foundation and other reputable OCD organizations publish educational materials and provider resources. Availability varies by country and region.

You do not need to discredit a therapist because they use another modality for another problem. The key question is what is being used as the specific treatment for OCD.

Protect Non-Treatment Time

A relationship cannot survive well if every interaction becomes symptom management.

Set periods where you do not review exposures, reassurance lapses, triggers, or accommodation charts unless something urgent needs attention.

Dinner can be dinner.

A walk can be a walk.

Sex does not have to become a treatment test.

A film does not have to become an exposure opportunity.

This is part of **ordinary life**.

If treatment has become the couple's only subject, schedule a short check-in rather than allowing it to expand indefinitely.

"Let's talk about the plan for fifteen minutes after dinner, then leave the rest of the evening alone."

That boundary protects both partners from turning the relationship into a clinic.

A Treatment-Role Worksheet

Use this page only if your partner is in treatment and wants you involved.

Area	My agreed role	Not my role
Reassurance	Use the agreed repeat-answer script	Judge whether every question is OCD
Checking	Stop one delegated check	Monitor whether my partner checks privately
ERP	Participate only in clinician-agreed tasks	Invent exposures
Medication	Support logistics if asked	Recommend doses or stopping
Homework	Encourage by request	Police completion
Sessions	Attend by mutual agreement	Demand confidential details

If there is no treatment, write "no clinician-directed role" across the top. Your accommodation limits can still apply, but you are not filling the treatment gap yourself.

Notice When Clinical Language Is Replacing Intimacy

A partner can learn so much about OCD that normal conversation starts sounding supervised.

"You are engaging in avoidance."

"That was reassurance seeking."

"Your distress is part of the cycle."

Even accurate terms can become distancing when they replace ordinary speech.

Try translating each clinical sentence back into relationship language.

"I think we are canceling because the fear is loud."

"I already answered that, and I do not want to answer it again."

"I know this is hard. I am going to keep the plan."

Use technical terms when they help you and your clinician communicate. Use human language when you are with the person you love.

The treatment role gets too large when you are always watching your partner through a clinical lens. One sign of healthy distance is that you can notice a symptom and still talk about the weather, work, dinner, music, or nothing important at all.

Do not make "good OCD management" the condition for warmth.

In a Nutshell

Learn enough about OCD treatment to understand the direction of change, then protect the boundary around who provides treatment.

A partner may have a useful role in ERP when a qualified clinician, the person with OCD, and the partner agree on that role. Keep it specific and limited. Do not design exposures, police homework, give medication advice, or diagnose every disagreement.

Your relationship needs room where nobody is the clinician.

Chapter 11 addresses the harder situation: your partner will not seek treatment, cannot access it, or has stopped trying.

Chapter 11: When They Will Not Get Help

Tessa had sent Amir three therapist directories, two articles, and the name of a specialist a friend recommended.

He did not call any of them.

When she brought it up again, Amir said therapy had made him worse before. Another time he said he could handle the checking himself. Another time he said the real problem was that Tessa had become less understanding.

Tessa kept researching because researching gave her something to do.

Eventually she had to confront the part no directory could solve: treatment belonged to Amir.

Her choices still belonged to her.

You Cannot Consent for Another Adult

A partner can encourage treatment, help with logistics, share information, offer to attend a session, and set boundaries around what they will participate in.

A partner cannot make another competent adult engage in psychotherapy.

That remains true when treatment would probably help.

It remains true when symptoms are disruptive.

It remains true when refusal is frustrating, frightening, or expensive.

NICE includes alternatives for adults who refuse or cannot engage with treatments that include ERP, such as considering OCD-adapted individual cognitive therapy. It also emphasizes collaborative care and appropriate family involvement. Those are clinical options, not tools a partner can impose. (National Institute for Health and Care Excellence, 2005)

The first shift is therefore from **How do I make them get help?** to **What can I change if they do not?**

Treatment Refusal Has More Than One Meaning

"Won't get help" can hide very different situations.

Your partner may not believe they have OCD.

They may accept the diagnosis but fear ERP.

They may have had a poor therapy experience.

They may be unable to find an OCD specialist.

They may face cost, insurance, transportation, language, disability, or childcare barriers.

They may be on a waiting list.

They may want medication but not therapy, or therapy but not medication.

They may have another condition that complicates treatment.

They may be ashamed of symptom content.

They may be ambivalent rather than fully opposed.

Ask before you assume.

"What makes treatment feel like a no right now?"

Listen for a practical barrier, a fear, a bad past experience, or a firm decision.

The answer changes what support is useful.

One Treatment Conversation Is Better Than Daily Persuasion

Repeated persuasion can become its own relationship ritual.

You mention therapy after every difficult evening.

Your partner defends why they do not need it.

You produce more evidence.

They produce more objections.

Neither person changes position, but the debate keeps returning.

Have one deliberate conversation.

Use four parts.

Observation: "The checking and reassurance are taking up a lot of our evenings and affecting my sleep."

Concern: "I don't think we can keep managing this only between us."

Invitation: "I would like you to get an assessment or treatment from someone who knows OCD. I will help with practical steps if you want."

Boundary: "Whether you do that is your choice. I am still going to stop doing the repeated checks and protect my sleep."

This respects autonomy while making the impact visible.

Avoid fake choices such as "Get therapy or else" unless the "or else" is a real boundary you are prepared to carry out.

Do Not Threaten What You Do Not Mean

A treatment ultimatum can briefly create movement because the stakes are high.

It can also damage credibility if you do not mean it.

"If you don't start therapy this week, I'm leaving."

If you are not prepared to leave, do not say it.

A genuine boundary is different.

"I cannot continue living with the children being required to participate in contamination rituals. We need that to change. I want professional help involved, and if the household cannot become safe and workable, I will have to make decisions about living arrangements."

That statement is serious because it describes your limit and consequence, not because it uses treatment as punishment.

You are allowed to decide that a relationship cannot continue under current conditions. You do not need to prove that your partner refused enough therapy first.

Reduce Your Accommodation Anyway

Treatment refusal does not obligate you to keep performing rituals.

You can still use the Support Pivot.

You can stop answering the same reassurance question.

You can stop delegated checking.

You can restore ordinary household choices that are genuinely yours to make.

You can protect sleep, time, work, and social plans.

The absence of treatment makes one boundary more important: do not slide into providing the missing treatment yourself.

You are changing your participation, not running ERP.

If your partner asks, "Then what am I supposed to do?" an honest answer may be:

"I don't know the best treatment step for you. That's why I want a professional involved. I know I won't keep doing the check."

That is more responsible than inventing an exposure because the specialist has not been called.

Offer Low-Friction Help Once

If the barrier is practical, make the first step easier without taking over indefinitely.

You might offer to sit beside your partner while they search a reputable provider directory.

You might call an insurer together.

You might help write three questions for a clinician.

You might provide transportation to an appointment.

You might attend the first session if invited.

You might help collect previous records.

Then stop.

If you make every call, choose the clinician, complete every form, arrange every appointment, remind repeatedly, and manage all follow-up, treatment-seeking itself can become another responsibility you carry for the relationship.

Support initiation without becoming the project manager unless that arrangement is genuinely necessary and mutually chosen.

Fear of ERP Deserves a Real Answer

Some people hear "exposure" and imagine being forced into their worst fear immediately.

A partner should not promise what treatment will look like for a specific person. You can direct the question toward a qualified OCD clinician.

A reasonable treatment interview asks how ERP is paced, how goals are chosen, how consent works, and what alternatives may be appropriate.

NHS guidance describes ERP as facing fears and obsessive thoughts without neutralizing them through compulsive behavior, often beginning with situations that cause less anxiety before more difficult ones. (NHS, 2023)

Use that as general education, not a guarantee about an individual plan.

If a previous therapist used coercive or poorly explained methods, do not dismiss the experience by saying "real ERP is supposed to be hard." Help your partner seek a clinician who can discuss what happened and what a new plan would involve.

"Therapy Does Not Work"

When your partner says therapy failed, ask what "therapy" means.

Was it OCD-focused CBT with ERP?

Was it supportive talk therapy for another problem?

How long did it last?

Was the clinician experienced with OCD?

Was treatment stopped because it was intolerable, inaccessible, ineffective, or interrupted?

You are not cross-examining your partner. You are separating a global conclusion from a specific history.

Then stop arguing.

"I hear that your last experience made you skeptical. I still think specialist input would help us. I won't keep trying to convince you every night."

A person can have valid reasons for distrust and still need more support than a partner can provide.

Medication Concerns Belong With Prescribers

If your partner refuses medication because of side effects, pregnancy concerns, previous reactions, or other medical issues, do not debate pharmacology from search results.

NHS and NICE both describe SSRIs as a treatment option for OCD, with clinical decisions depending on individual circumstances and severity. (National Institute for Health and Care Excellence, 2005; NHS, 2023)

Your role can be logistical and relational.

"Would you tell the prescriber exactly what happened last time?"

"Do you want me in the appointment?"

"I won't tell you what dose to take."

If medication is prescribed, changes and discontinuation should be discussed with the appropriate clinician.

Get Your Own Support

You do not need your partner's participation to seek support for yourself.

That may be individual therapy, a support group, a trusted family member, practical legal or financial advice where relevant, or an OCD-family education resource.

Your own clinician should not treat your absent partner by proxy. The useful work is about your boundaries, stress, decisions, safety, and relationship patterns.

Bring concrete questions.

"How do I stop arguing after I set a limit?"

"What is a reasonable sleep boundary?"

"How do I decide whether the children are being affected?"

"I am considering separation. What do I need to think through?"

"How do I distinguish fear from actual safety concerns?"

This moves you from waiting for your partner to change into clarifying what you can do.

When Refusal and Coercion Become Entangled

A person has the right to refuse treatment.

They do not have the right to force you to perform rituals through intimidation.

"If you loved me, you would check" is pressure.

"If you do not check, I will destroy your things" is a threat.

Blocking your exit, controlling money, isolating you, threatening children or pets, or using self-harm threats to force compliance requires a safety lens.

Do not let an OCD diagnosis make coercive behavior disappear.

OCD can contribute to intense distress around accommodation. It does not make you responsible for accepting abuse.

Make a No-Treatment Plan

If your partner says no to treatment for now, write a plan for *your* side.

My accommodation targets: Which two behaviors will I reduce?

My non-negotiables: What must remain safe and workable for me, children, or dependents?

My own support: Who can I speak to regularly?

My practical protections: What do I need around sleep, work, money, transport, privacy, or living arrangements?

My review date: When will I reassess whether the relationship is workable under these conditions?

A review date is not a secret deadline designed to frighten your partner. It is a commitment to stop living in indefinite postponement.

If They Later Choose Help

Do not turn the decision into a victory speech.

"You finally listened to me" creates a new hierarchy.

Use ordinary support.

"Good. What would be helpful from me?"

Then remember Chapter 10. Treatment beginning does not mean you take over.

A professional plan may ask you to change accommodation in more structured ways. It may also reveal that some things you thought were OCD are not.

Stay teachable.

Decide What Would Count as Movement

If your partner refuses full treatment, do not let the only acceptable outcome be "starts ERP immediately."

Movement can be smaller.

They agree to an assessment.

They read one reputable source.

They allow you to stop one delegated check.

They talk honestly about the cost to the relationship.

They ask a primary-care clinician about options.

They return to a previous therapist to discuss what went badly.

They consent to one partner session.

These steps are not equivalent to treatment, and some may never lead to treatment. They can still tell you whether the household is capable of collaborative change.

Your boundary should not depend on movement appearing. But noticing movement can keep you from treating a complicated decision as simple defiance.

Likewise, repeated promises without action are information. If "I will get help soon" has postponed the same conversation for a year, set a review date based on what you need rather than on the next promise.

In a Nutshell

You cannot make another adult accept treatment. You can make one clear invitation, help with practical barriers, and stop turning persuasion into a nightly argument.

Whether treatment happens or not, your behavior, safety, sleep, money, time, parenting, and relationship choices remain yours.

Set accommodation limits without becoming the missing therapist. Seek your own support. If the relationship has become unsafe or coercive, respond to that problem directly.

Chapter 12 turns to a particularly difficult content area: when OCD asks the relationship itself to provide endless certainty.

Chapter 12: When OCD Targets the Relationship

Grace had answered versions of the same question for months.

"Do you still love me?"

"Yes."

"Are you sure?"

"Yes."

"Do you ever wonder if we're wrong for each other?"

"Everyone wonders sometimes."

"So you do wonder."

Then came comparison questions, attraction questions, memory questions, questions about tone, sex, arguments, past partners, imagined futures, and whether Grace's hesitation before answering meant something.

The subject was the relationship, so refusing to discuss it felt absurd.

The task was not to stop talking about the relationship. It was to stop turning the relationship into an instrument for certainty.

Real Relationships Contain Real Doubt

A healthy relationship is not a state of permanent certainty.

Partners get irritated. Attraction varies. People notice other people. Values line up imperfectly. Some arguments matter. Some incompatibilities are real. People change. Relationships sometimes end.

That reality makes relationship-centered OCD difficult for couples because the feared subject is not imaginary. The compulsion can attach to a question no partner can answer with absolute certainty.

"How do I know I love you enough?"

"How do I know you are the right person?"

"How do I know that attraction means nothing?"

"How do I know our argument was normal?"

"How do I know I won't leave someday?"

The partner is tempted to provide a guarantee that love itself cannot provide.

Do not make the opposite mistake and treat every relationship concern as OCD. Genuine problems remain genuine.

The goal is to distinguish **relationship problem-solving** from **relationship certainty seeking**.

Three Lanes for Relationship Conversations

Use three lanes.

Connection includes affection, ordinary reassurance, sexual communication, sharing appreciation, talking about hopes, and asking for closeness.

Problem-solving includes a specific issue with a specific decision or repair. "We keep fighting about money. We need a budget." "I felt dismissed when you interrupted me. I want us to handle that differently."

Certainty seeking includes repeated tests that ask the relationship to prove an unprovable conclusion. "Tell me again that we are definitely right for each other." "Compare me with your ex one more time." "Review your feelings until you can promise they never change."

A single conversation can move between lanes.

Grace may say, "I was hurt that you canceled our anniversary plan." That is a relationship problem.

Luis may apologize and suggest another plan.

Then he asks, "Does the fact that I forgot mean I don't love you enough?" The conversation has shifted into meaning-certainty.

Grace can address both.

"We need to repair the anniversary issue. I don't want to keep deciding what the mistake proves about your whole capacity to love me."

That is **process not proof** applied to relationship content.

Ordinary Reassurance Is Not Forbidden

The phrase "never reassure" can damage intimacy if applied mechanically.

Partners say "I love you." They say "We're okay." They say "I still want to be here." They comfort each other after conflict. They confirm commitments.

You do not need to remove those acts to be non-accommodating.

Look at pattern and function.

Does the reassurance arise naturally, or is it demanded repeatedly until it feels exactly right?

Can the answer stand?

Does a new detail immediately reopen the question?

Are you being asked to inspect your feelings, memories, attraction, or future for certainty?

Has your partner developed tests, comparisons, confession requests, or rules for how you must answer?

If yes, the repeated certainty process is the target.

You are allowed to keep saying "I love you" because you mean it. You are also allowed to say, "I don't want 'I love you' to become a test I have to pass every ten minutes."

Confession Can Recruit the Partner

Some OCD patterns involve repeated confession.

Your partner may feel compelled to tell you every intrusive thought, every moment of attraction, every memory, every possible mistake, every detail that could be interpreted as dishonest.

The confession often comes with a question.

"Are you angry?"

"Does this change what you think of me?"

"Would you leave someone who thought that?"

"Do I need to tell you more?"

Honesty matters in relationships. Compulsive disclosure is different from ordinary honesty because it is driven by the need to neutralize guilt or uncertainty and may repeat beyond what is relevant.

You can set a limit without demanding secrecy.

"If there is information that affects our agreements or choices, I need honesty. I don't need every intrusive thought reported to me."

"I don't want to be the person who decides whether each thought needs confession."

"If you are unsure whether disclosure is part of a compulsion, that is a good treatment question."

If the disclosed information concerns actual abuse, infidelity, financial harm, safety, or another material relationship issue, do not dismiss it as OCD. Deal with the real issue.

Attraction Questions Are a Common Trap

"Did you think they were attractive?"

"More attractive than me?"

"How long did you look?"

"Did you imagine being with them?"

"Did you feel something?"

A partner may answer because the questions seem to concern trust.

Trust can require real conversations about boundaries. Repeated attraction interrogation is something else.

Separate the agreement from the test.

"We can talk about what fidelity means to us. I won't report every attraction or prove what each glance meant."

This sentence preserves the relationship's right to agreements while refusing surveillance.

The same principle applies in reverse. A person with OCD may repeatedly inspect their own attraction to the partner and ask for reassurance about whether fluctuations mean the relationship is wrong. The non-OCD partner should not become the evaluator of whether those feelings are "normal enough."

Sex Needs Consent, Not Exposure Logic

Relationship OCD and contamination fears can affect sexual intimacy.

This area requires a firm boundary: no partner owes sexual contact as an exposure exercise.

A clinician-guided treatment plan may address intimacy-related avoidance with the person's consent, but relationship consent remains specific, voluntary, and revocable.

Do not say, "You need to have sex because avoidance feeds OCD."

Do not use affection as a test either.

"Kiss me so I know you still love me" can turn intimacy into reassurance.

Partners can discuss sex as a relationship issue:

"I miss sexual closeness."

"I don't want sex to be governed entirely by contamination rules."

"I also don't want either of us doing sexual things to prove anything."

A couples therapist may help with the relationship dimension, while OCD-specific treatment addresses compulsions. One is not a substitute for the other.

Set a Time Boundary on Relationship Analysis

Some couples lose entire evenings to the relationship autopsy.

"How did you feel when we met?"

"Was it stronger than now?"

"What did you mean when you said 'fine'?"

"Would you remarry me?"

"Do you ever picture being single?"

A useful boundary is to move genuine relationship work into a planned window.

"We can talk for thirty minutes tomorrow about the argument and what we want to change. I won't spend tonight answering questions about whether the relationship is definitely right."

The time boundary does not tell your partner not to have thoughts. It protects the couple from unlimited analysis.

If a real problem requires more than thirty minutes, schedule more time or seek relationship support. The key is that the conversation has an agenda other than obtaining certainty.

When You Are the One With Real Doubt

This book is written to partners of people with OCD, but you may have doubts of your own.

You may be unsure whether you want to stay.

That matters.

Do not hide genuine uncertainty behind an OCD script because you fear triggering symptoms.

If Luis asks Grace, "Are we okay?" and Grace is actually considering separation, saying "I won't reassure your OCD" would avoid an important truth.

She can say, "I am not ready to make a final decision tonight, but I do have real concerns about the relationship that we need to discuss."

Then set a structure for that discussion.

Your partner's OCD does not require you to provide false certainty about your feelings.

Honesty can be compassionate and difficult at the same time.

Do Not Use Breakup Threats as Anti-Reassurance

The opposite error is weaponizing uncertainty.

"Maybe I will leave. You need to learn to tolerate uncertainty."

That is not a Support Pivot if you are saying it to provoke exposure.

Relationship decisions have consequences. Speak with the amount of certainty you genuinely have.

"I am committed to working on this relationship, and I cannot guarantee the future."

"I am considering whether I can stay if the household does not change."

"I am not planning to leave, and I won't keep answering the same question tonight."

These statements are different because they report your actual position.

Create a Relationship Conversation Sort

For one week, mark five relationship conversations after they happen.

Conversation	Connection	Problem-solvin g	Certainty seeking	What response would fit next time?
Asked for hug after hard day	Yes	No	No	Give affection if wanted
Argued about spending	No	Yes	Maybe	Make budget plan
Asked 8 times if I still love them	Some	No	Yes	Ordinary affection, no repeated test
Confessed intrusive thought	Maybe	No	Yes if repeated	Do not issue moral verdict
Discussed sex frequency	Yes	Yes	No	Continue real conversation

Do not show the table as evidence that your partner is "doing OCD." Use it to train your own discrimination.

What to Say in the Live Moment

For repeated love questions:

"I've answered from my heart. I don't want to turn it into a certainty test."

For repeated compatibility questions:

"We can discuss actual problems we want to solve. I won't keep deciding whether we are perfectly matched."

For comparison:

"I'm not going to rank you against someone else."

For confession:

"If this changes something real between us, tell me. I don't want every intrusive thought brought to me for clearance."

For your own real concern:

"I do have something real to discuss. Let's make time for that instead of trying to get certainty right now."

Plain sentences protect the distinction better than jargon.

When Relationship Therapy Helps

Couple therapy may be useful for communication, trust, division of labor, intimacy, conflict, or decisions about staying together. It should not be presented as a proven substitute for OCD-specific treatment. NICE notes a lack of convincing evidence for marital or couple therapy as a specific treatment for OCD. (National Institute for Health and Care Excellence, 2005)

If you seek couple therapy, ask whether the clinician understands OCD and family accommodation. Otherwise, a well-intentioned therapist may encourage repeated reassurance or treat every OCD-driven certainty demand as a standard communication need.

The best fit may involve coordination between relationship work and OCD treatment, with clear consent and privacy boundaries.

Protect Positive Relationship Rituals

When you reduce certainty rituals, keep the rituals that make you a couple.

A goodbye kiss.

A weekly meal.

A private joke.

A message after a difficult day.

Celebrating an anniversary.

Saying "I love you" when you want to say it.

The distinction is function, not repetition alone. A nightly affectionate phrase chosen freely is not the same as a phrase that must be repeated until it produces the correct feeling.

If a positive ritual starts to acquire rules about exact wording, timing, number, or emotional certainty, talk about that change.

"I want our goodnight to stay ours. I do not want to repeat it until it feels perfect."

Accommodation reduction should create more room for spontaneous connection, not make the relationship afraid of tenderness.

In a Nutshell

When OCD targets the relationship, you do not solve it by refusing all reassurance or by pretending the relationship has no real problems.

Sort conversations into connection, problem-solving, and certainty seeking. Keep affection and honest relationship work. Reduce repeated testing, comparison, confession, and guarantees that cannot stand.

Do not use sex, breakup threats, or false certainty as treatment tools.

A relationship with OCD still needs to be a relationship, not a diagnostic exercise.

Chapter 13 widens the lens to children, relatives, and friends who can be pulled into accommodation without choosing that role.

Chapter 13: Protect the Rest of the Family

Nia realized the children had learned the rules better than she had.

Their daughter knew which side of the hallway to use after school. Their son knew not to ask Owen whether he wanted help with the door because the answer could lead to a checking sequence. Both children knew how to answer "Did you touch that?" quickly and confidently.

Nobody had sat them down and assigned these jobs.

They had adapted.

Family accommodation can spread through a household until children, relatives, and friends are participating in symptoms they barely understand.

The partner's task is not only to reduce their own accommodation. It is also to stop outsourcing it.

Children Should Not Carry Adult Certainty

Children often notice distress before adults realize they are watching.

A child may start answering reassurance questions because the fastest route back to calm is obvious.

"Yes, Dad, the door is locked."

"No, Mom, I didn't touch it."

"I promise I washed."

"Nothing bad happened at school."

The child may feel helpful. They may also learn that another person's distress depends on providing the correct answer.

NICE recommends that assessment consider the impact of rituals and compulsions on others, particularly dependent children, and the degree to which family members are involved in OCD-related behavior. (National Institute for Health and Care Excellence, 2005)

That does not tell you exactly how to parent in your home. It does establish that children's involvement is clinically relevant, not a side issue.

Remove the Job Without Making the Child the Expert

If your child has become a reassurance provider, do not give them a lecture on reinforcement.

Use simple language.

"You do not have to answer the same checking question again."

"That is a grown-up problem. You can come back to your game."

"You are not in charge of making Dad feel certain."

"You do not have to wash again because someone asks. Come tell me if you are confused about a house rule."

Keep the adult boundary with the adult.

Do not say, "Tell Mom that is her OCD and refuse." That makes the child the treatment enforcer.

If the person with OCD asks the child again, you can intervene.

"I'll handle this. The kids are not going to do checking questions."

You may still have to protect the child from the interaction even if your partner disagrees.

Keep Explanations Age Appropriate

Children deserve enough information to understand that the situation is not their responsibility.

A younger child may hear:

"Sometimes Dad's brain gets stuck on a worry and asks for the same answer again. Grown-ups are helping with that. You do not have to fix the worry."

An older child may understand OCD by name:

"OCD can make uncertainty feel very urgent. Repeated reassurance can become part of the pattern. You can answer ordinary questions, but you are not responsible for doing rituals or repeated certainty checks."

Do not share intimate symptom content the child does not need.

Do not ask the child to keep secrets about behavior that frightens them.

Make it clear whom they can go to if they are worried.

Grandparents and Relatives Can Become the Backup System

When a partner reduces accommodation, the request may migrate.

Marcus stops answering Priya's contamination question, so Priya calls her mother.

Elena stops checking Jonah's messages, so he asks his sister.

Amir's parents follow house rules Tessa is trying to reduce because they want peace.

You cannot control other adults' choices. You can stop recruiting them yourself.

Do not call a relative to obtain reassurance on your partner's behalf.

Do not ask a grandparent to enforce a ritual with children.

Do not secretly tell family members to "stand firm" as though they are a treatment team.

Where disclosure is welcome, use a simple consistent explanation.

"We are trying to reduce repeated checking and reassurance. Please do not answer the same certainty question over and over. You can be warm and change the subject."

If your partner does not consent to diagnostic disclosure, keep privacy.

"You do not need to repeat the answer. We are working on some household boundaries."

Privacy does not require you to instruct others to participate in a ritual.

Friends Need Permission to Stay Friends

Friends can be pulled into accommodation through texts, calls, social plans, and reassurance.

"Can you ask her whether I offended her?"

"Tell him I did not mean it that way."

"Please check whether the restaurant is safe enough."

"Can you promise you are not upset?"

If you become the intermediary, you are participating in the loop.

Encourage direct ordinary communication when a real relationship issue exists.

"If you think you need to repair something with your friend, you can send one normal message. I won't poll them to find out whether you're definitely okay."

The friend can then decide how to respond.

Avoid telling friends that they must ignore your partner. The goal is not social isolation. It is to keep relationships from becoming a distributed certainty network.

Co-Parenting Requires an Adult Agreement

OCD can create disagreements over what children are allowed to do.

Can they play outside?

Can friends visit?

How much washing is required?

Can they touch the family pet?

Can they sleep away from home?

Can they take public transport?

Can they use the kitchen?

One parent may frame the rules as safety. The other may see accommodation.

These decisions deserve more care than a one-line script because the child cannot choose freely between two conflicting household systems.

When possible, write down the ordinary parenting standard using credible health, school, or safety guidance where relevant. If disagreement is severe or persistent, seek professional help. An OCD-informed family clinician can help distinguish symptom accommodation from reasonable parenting concerns.

Do not deliberately expose a child to something to treat a parent's OCD. The child is not a therapeutic prop.

Protect School and Daily Function

A child's routine may bend around a parent's symptoms.

They arrive late because leaving requires checking.

They miss activities because transportation routes are restricted.

They avoid bringing friends home.

They participate in laundry or cleaning rituals.

They learn not to touch a parent.

They stay quiet because questions after bedtime wake the household.

One incident may be manageable. A pattern deserves attention.

Use a **dependent impact check** once a month if children live in the home.

Area	Question
School	Is OCD-related delay, absence, or checking affecting attendance or homework?
Friends	Can the child invite and visit friends without ritual participation?
Sleep	Is the child regularly kept awake by rituals or conflict?
Body autonomy	Is the child required to wash, change, confess, or avoid touch beyond ordinary standards?
Responsibility	Is the child asked to reassure, check, monitor, or calm the adult?
Fear	Is the child afraid of the adult's response to mistakes or boundary changes?
Activities	Are hobbies, travel, meals, or family outings repeatedly restricted?

If several areas are impaired, this is bigger than one accommodation target.

Seek appropriate family, pediatric, school, or mental-health support depending on the problem.

Keep Adult Conflict Away From Children Where You Can

Accommodation arguments can recruit children as witnesses.

"Tell your father this is unreasonable."

"You know Mom checked the door, right?"

"Ask the kids who is causing the problem."

Do not make a child vote on whether a fear is true.

If the disagreement happens in front of them, repair the exposure to conflict.

"You heard us arguing about a house rule. That was an adult disagreement. You do not have to decide who was right, and you are not responsible for fixing it."

If high-conflict episodes are frequent, your family may need more support than a self-help plan can provide.

Extended Family May Have Different Beliefs

One relative may think your partner needs more discipline.

Another may think every accommodation is kindness.

Another may deny OCD.

Another may be terrified of upsetting anyone.

You do not need consensus.

Give relatives only the information necessary for their role.

"We are not doing repeated reassurance questions at dinner."

"The children are not participating in washing rituals."

"If you want to help, please keep the visit normal."

Do not stage a family intervention unless a qualified professional has recommended and structured one.

Shame rarely improves cooperation.

Privacy Versus Protection

Partners can feel trapped between protecting diagnostic privacy and explaining strange household rules.

Use the least disclosure necessary.

A babysitter does not need symptom history. They need clear instructions about the child's routine and safety.

A teacher may need to know that family circumstances are affecting lateness, but not intimate OCD content unless the family chooses to share it.

A grandparent caring for children may need to know not to require an extra washing sequence.

If there is abuse, credible danger, or a child-protection concern, privacy is not the only value. Follow applicable law and seek professional advice.

This book cannot determine reporting obligations in your jurisdiction.

When Your Partner Says You Are Turning the Family Against Them

That accusation can land hard.

Do not answer by building a case.

"I don't want anyone against you. I am trying to keep the kids out of reassurance and checking."

If they object to diagnostic disclosure, listen.

"We can agree on what we tell people. I still won't ask the children to do rituals."

If they object to the boundary itself, keep the conversation adult.

"The kids' role is not negotiable for me. We can get professional help deciding how to handle the household."

Your partner can disagree with your interpretation. Children still need protection from adult responsibilities.

Create a Simple Family Response

A family response should be short enough that everyone knows it.

For example:

Adults answer an ordinary practical question once.

Children are never asked to repeat reassurance.

Children do not perform adult checking.

Visitors are not recruited into rituals.

Real safety concerns go to the appropriate adult or professional.

That is enough.

Do not make the home display a clinical poster unless everyone wants one. The aim is predictable behavior, not branding the family around OCD.

Give Children a Way to Opt Out

A child who has been part of rituals may not know that refusal is allowed.

Give them one neutral sentence.

"I need a grown-up."

They can use it when asked to check, reassure, wash again, inspect, or settle an adult question.

The child does not have to identify OCD.

They do not have to challenge the parent.

They simply transfer the request to another adult.

Tell them in advance that they will not be punished for using the sentence.

Then make sure an adult actually responds. If the child says "I need a grown-up" and is sent back to manage the distressed parent, the protection is only verbal.

For older children, invite questions without asking them to monitor symptoms.

"What parts of the house rules are hard for you?"

"Is there anything you are being asked to do that makes you uncomfortable?"

Listen for practical impact before offering explanations.

A child's job is to be a child in the family, not the most available nervous system.

In a Nutshell

Accommodation spreads easily because families want to help and children adapt quickly.

Protect children from reassurance, checking, monitoring, and ritual roles. Keep explanations age appropriate. Do not make relatives a substitute treatment team. Preserve privacy where possible without using privacy as a reason to keep others trapped in compulsions.

If OCD is significantly affecting a child's safety, sleep, school, social life, or body autonomy, seek professional support.

Chapter 14 turns back to you. Reducing accommodation is incomplete if OCD still owns your schedule, attention, money, and identity.

Chapter 14: Get Your Own Life Back

Simone had become excellent at being available.

She could answer Caleb from work without leaving a meeting. She knew which groceries were acceptable, which routes were difficult, which relatives needed advance instructions, and which evenings were likely to run late because of checking.

When a friend asked what she had been doing for herself, Simone listed household tasks.

The answer startled her more than the question.

Accommodation is not only what you do during a ritual. It can also be the life you stop having so that you are always ready to prevent the next one.

Your Life Is Not Collateral

Partners often wait for OCD to improve before restoring their own plans.

"When treatment is working, I'll see friends again."

"When the checking is shorter, I'll go back to the gym."

"When they can tolerate being home by themselves, I'll travel."

"When the contamination rules ease, I'll have people over."

Sometimes sequencing is sensible. Sometimes waiting becomes indefinite.

The International OCD Foundation's family guidance explicitly notes the importance of separate time and maintaining family routines rather than allowing OCD to run everybody's life. (Van Noppen & Pato, 2009)

You do not need to earn personal time by first solving your partner's symptoms.

Accommodation Can Hide as Availability

You may not wash, check, or reassure very much. You may still organize yourself around being reachable.

You keep your phone on during meetings.

You avoid alcohol at dinner because you may need to drive home.

You decline overnight trips.

You do not take a long shower because a question may come.

You arrange work around appointments you are not required to attend.

You sleep lightly because checking may start.

You stay close enough to intervene if distress rises.

Some of this may be necessary for a period, especially during genuine illness or crisis. The question is whether temporary support has become the permanent architecture of your life.

Audit Six Personal Domains

Look at six domains without mentioning your partner's behavior.

Sleep. How many nights per week do OCD-related conversations, checking, or routines delay or interrupt your sleep?

Work. How often do you alter hours, take calls, leave early, miss opportunities, or conceal strain?

Money. What costs do you personally absorb because of avoidance, replacement, transport, cleaning, appointments, or reduced work?

Friendships and family. Whom have you stopped seeing or inviting?

Privacy and solitude. Can you be unavailable for ordinary periods without a crisis?

Interests and body. What exercise, hobbies, sex, rest, spiritual practice, or leisure has disappeared?

Use actual examples. "I have no life" is emotionally understandable but difficult to act on. "I have canceled Wednesday choir six times in two months because the evening checking runs late" gives you a restoration target.

Resentment Is Data, Not Instructions

Resentment often frightens caring partners.

You may think that feeling resentful means you have become unkind.

Resentment can also indicate that a limit, division of labor, or need has been ignored for too long.

Do not let resentment make decisions by itself. It can push you toward contempt, scorekeeping, or explosive withdrawal.

Use it as a prompt.

"What am I repeatedly doing that I no longer consent to?"

"What do I need that has not been named?"

"Which accommodation has the largest cost to my ordinary life?"

"What relationship issue am I calling OCD because I do not know how to address it directly?"

The answer may be a boundary, a practical renegotiation, professional support, or a larger decision about the relationship.

Protect Sleep Early

Sleep loss makes every other skill harder.

A common pattern is the bedtime reassurance loop. The lights go off. A doubt arrives. One question becomes twenty minutes. The partner keeps answering because refusing seems likely to create a longer conflict.

Set a sleep boundary outside bedtime.

"After eleven, I won't do repeated OCD questions or checking. If there is a real emergency, wake me. Otherwise, we can talk in the morning."

Define *real emergency* by ordinary standards, not by how intense the anxiety feels.

If your partner repeatedly wakes you despite the boundary, you may need a practical plan: separate sleeping space for a period, earplugs if safe, or professional support around household functioning.

Do not use sleep deprivation as a treatment strategy for either person.

Separate Money From Reassurance

OCD can have financial consequences.

Repeated replacement of "contaminated" items.

Medical consultations used mainly for reassurance.

Taxi costs from avoided routes.

Lost bookings.

Specialized cleaning.

Missed work.

Duplicate purchases.

The partner may quietly absorb these costs because arguing seems worse.

Make shared money visible.

Use a monthly category called "OCD-related accommodation costs" for your private planning if that helps you see the pattern. Do not use the number to shame your partner.

Then set practical limits around spending you control.

"I won't replace a household item that is functional solely because it feels contaminated."

"Shared purchases over this amount require both of us to agree."

"I won't pay repeated cancellation fees for plans I still intend to attend."

If money is controlled, hidden, or used coercively, seek financial or legal advice appropriate to your location. This book cannot resolve ownership or legal-rights questions.

Restore Two Non-OCD Commitments

Choose two recurring commitments that matter to you and are not organized around symptom management.

A weekly class.

Dinner with a friend.

A run.

A family phone call.

A volunteer shift.

A quiet morning at the library.

A religious service.

A hobby night.

Put them on the calendar first.

The commitment should be small enough that you can keep it.

Tell your partner what you are doing without asking permission where permission is not required.

"I'm going to my class Thursday. I won't be available for reassurance calls from seven to nine. If there is a real emergency, text 'emergency' and tell me what happened."

Be careful with the emergency channel. If every distress spike becomes an emergency, the boundary needs clarification.

Being Unavailable Is a Skill

Partners can become trained to respond within seconds.

Start with ordinary unavailability.

Put the phone on Do Not Disturb during a meeting.

Take a walk without live reassurance texting.

Read in another room for thirty minutes.

Let a nonurgent message wait.

Your partner may dislike it. You may dislike it more because your own anxiety rises when you do not know whether they are distressed.

That is worth noticing.

Accommodation can be maintained by the non-OCD partner's need to restore calm too.

You do not need to label your own anxiety as pathological. You need to stop letting it decide every response.

Keep Friendship From Becoming a Complaint Department

You need people who know you as more than someone's partner.

But when relationships are under strain, every friendship can turn into a debrief.

Choose at least one interaction where you do not discuss OCD unless something major has happened.

See a film.

Talk about work.

Cook.

Watch a game.

Go somewhere neither of you associates with the disorder.

This is not denial. It is restoration.

If you need intensive support, therapy or a support group may be better suited to detailed processing than one friend who becomes your only outlet.

Privacy Is Part of Your Life Too

Some partners lose privacy because they are expected to report where they were, whom they saw, what they thought, what they touched, what they spent, or how they felt.

Some of those questions may be part of OCD. Some may be relationship control.

You are allowed to have ordinary privacy.

That does not mean secrecy about shared agreements.

It means you do not have to produce an exhaustive log of internal experience to neutralize someone else's uncertainty.

A privacy boundary might be:

"I will tell you anything that affects our relationship agreements. I won't report every person I noticed today."

"I will share the household account. I won't submit screenshots of every purchase for repeated checking."

"I will tell you my plan. I won't keep proving where I am through messages."

If refusing creates fear of retaliation, use a safety lens.

Burnout Is Not a Diagnostic Label Here

You may describe yourself as burned out. This book does not diagnose a disorder from exhaustion, resentment, or overload.

Treat the word as a signal to examine capacity.

How many hours of sleep are you getting?

How much uninterrupted work time?

How many caregiving tasks?

How many other stressors?

How much support?

Which responsibilities can be reduced?

Which accommodations can stop?

What health care do *you* need?

Seek medical or mental-health care if your own symptoms require it.

The partner is not less deserving of professional support because the other person has the named diagnosis.

When Getting Your Life Back Changes the Relationship

Restoration can reveal difficult truths.

You may discover your partner adapts better than you expected.

You may discover conflict increases but becomes manageable.

You may discover that the relationship had very little room for your independent life even before OCD.

You may discover you do not want to return to the old arrangement.

Do not force these findings into a positive story.

The purpose of restoring ordinary life is to give both people better information about what the relationship can hold.

If independence itself is treated as betrayal, that is a relationship issue that deserves direct attention.

Make a Partner Life Budget

A budget is a limit on scarce resources.

Use four resources: time, attention, money, and sleep.

Resource	Current OCD-related cost	Limit I want	First change
Time	6 hours/week reassurance	2 planned check-ins plus live limits	End repeat questions

Resource	Current OCD-related cost	Limit I want	First change
Attention	Messages during work	No nonurgent response during meetings	Do Not Disturb
Money	Replacement items	Shared cap, no automatic replacement	Pause 24 hours
Sleep	3 late-night loops/week	No repeated questions after 11	Bedtime script

Do not turn the numbers into a scorecard against your partner.

They are evidence for your own planning.

Rebuild Capacity Before You Spend It

When partners finally set limits, they often use the new time immediately for more problem-solving.

You finish a reassurance conversation in five minutes instead of forty and spend the saved thirty minutes researching therapists.

You stop a checking ritual and use the evening to redesign the household plan.

That can keep your life centered on OCD even while accommodation falls.

Spend some recovered capacity on something that does not improve anyone.

Read a novel.

Cook because you like the food.

Sit outside.

Fix something unrelated.

Watch a match.

Do nothing useful.

This is not a technique for becoming more patient later. It is ordinary ownership of time.

If leisure produces guilt, notice the thought without obeying it. Being available every minute is not proof of love.

Recovery on the partner side includes periods in which you are not learning about OCD, managing OCD, recovering from OCD, or preparing to discuss OCD.

Put one such period on the calendar this week and protect it as seriously as an appointment.

Reclaim One Decision You Used to Delegate

Availability is not the only thing accommodation can take. It can also take decision-making.

You may have stopped choosing the restaurant, route, weekend plan, purchase, or bedtime because the negotiation around OCD was exhausting.

Choose one low-stakes decision you want to participate in again.

"We will alternate who chooses takeout."

"I am choosing the route when I drive."

"I am setting my own bedtime."

"I will decide whether my clothes need washing by the ordinary standard we agreed."

The purpose is not to win a power contest. It is to re-enter shared life as a person with preferences.

If every independent choice produces punishment, intimidation, or threats, treat that pattern as a relationship-safety issue rather than a boundary-skills problem.

A relationship affected by OCD can still contain two adults who sometimes want different things.

In a Nutshell

Accommodation can shrink your life even when you are not actively performing a ritual.

Audit sleep, work, money, relationships, privacy, and interests. Restore two recurring commitments. Practice ordinary unavailability. Set limits on the resources you control.

Your life does not have to wait in storage until someone else's OCD improves.

Part IV begins with the question that makes many partners afraid to reduce accommodation at all: what if the fear is real?

Part IV: Keep Safety and Recovery in View

Chapter 15: Know What Counts as Safety

Maya's first instinct was to refuse the check.

Daniel had called from the car and asked her to go back into the kitchen. The day before, they had agreed that Maya would no longer inspect the stove after Daniel had already done the ordinary check.

Then he said, "I smell gas."

That was new information.

Maya did not answer with "process not proof." She treated the situation as a possible real-world hazard and followed the appropriate safety response.

The principle is simple: **not every urgent request is OCD, and not every distress spike is danger**.

You need a way to tell the difference without pretending you can eliminate uncertainty.

Use the Safety Screen Before the Accommodation Rule

A **safety screen** is a check for genuine medical, violence, self-harm, dependent-safety, or emergency concerns before treating a request as an OCD loop.

Ask five questions.

Is there new objective information? A gas odor, an alarm, an injury, a medication error, a child missing, smoke, a new severe symptom, a credible threat.

Is there a recognized safety procedure? A fire alarm has a procedure. Medication errors have professional channels. Child-safety concerns have adult and, when appropriate, professional responses.

Is the request about repeating a completed procedure, or doing the procedure for the first time? One ordinary check may be appropriate. Ten checks after completion may be compulsive.

Would I respond this way if OCD were not part of the relationship? This helps reveal whether you are underreacting because you fear accommodation or overreacting because distress is loud.

Do I need professional judgment rather than a partner judgment? Medical, psychiatric, legal, and safety-critical questions often belong outside the relationship.

If the screen points to real risk, respond to the risk. If it points to repeated certainty seeking after an ordinary response is complete, use your accommodation plan.

Intensity Is Not the Same as Danger

OCD-related distress can look urgent.

Your partner may say, "I can't handle this."

They may cry, pace, plead, become angry, or report intense physical anxiety.

Those reactions matter. They do not automatically establish that the feared catastrophe is occurring.

Likewise, a calm presentation does not prove safety.

The safety screen focuses on facts, threats, function, and appropriate procedures, not on volume.

This protects against two opposite errors.

The first is treating every intense OCD episode as an emergency, which can feed repeated reassurance and emergency-service use.

The second is dismissing real danger because "they always worry."

A history of OCD does not make a person immune to real illness, accidents, abuse, or crisis.

Medical Concerns Need Ordinary Medical Channels

Health-themed OCD can produce repeated symptom checks, internet searches, appointment requests, and questions to partners.

A partner should not decide that a symptom is "just OCD" when medical evaluation is appropriate.

Use the medical plan available to you.

If a clinician has given specific red-flag instructions, follow them.

If a symptom is new, severe, rapidly changing, or otherwise concerning, seek appropriate medical advice.

If the same stable concern has already been evaluated and the request is to repeat the same reassurance without new information, your accommodation limit may apply.

A useful sentence is:

"We followed the medical advice for this situation. If one of the things they told us to watch for happens, we will act. I won't keep rechecking the same symptom now."

Do not invent thresholds from this book.

Medication Questions Are Safety-Sensitive

Medication is a poor place for partner improvisation.

If your partner asks, "Did I take this already?" there may be a real risk of double dosing. The correct response depends on the medication and circumstances.

Use the prescribed system, pharmacist, poison-control service, prescriber, or other appropriate medical guidance. Do not guess in order to avoid "reassurance."

Similarly, do not advise a partner to skip, double, stop, or taper medication based on OCD principles.

Once the real medication issue is resolved through the proper channel, repeated requests to certify certainty can be handled separately.

Safety first, accommodation second.

Self-Harm Statements Require a Different Response

OCD can include unwanted intrusive thoughts or images about self-harm, but OCD is also associated with clinically important rates of suicidal ideation and suicide attempts. A partner should not infer intent, or the absence of intent, from an OCD label or symptom theme. (Pellegrini et al., 2020)

If your partner talks about wanting to die, wanting to harm themselves, being unable to stay safe, having a plan or intent, or taking steps toward self-harm, take it seriously and seek appropriate professional or emergency help.

You are not responsible for performing a formal risk assessment.

Do not respond to a credible self-harm statement by saying, "I won't reassure you."

Do not agree to keep imminent risk secret.

If you are unsure and the concern seems significant, use professional crisis support.

After a qualified assessment clarifies that a particular repeated question is part of OCD, a clinician can help you understand your role.

Intrusive Harm Thoughts Are Not Yours to Diagnose

Some people with OCD have unwanted intrusive thoughts about harming others and may repeatedly ask for reassurance that they are not dangerous.

That pattern is well recognized in OCD. It is also true that a partner cannot determine risk from symptom theme alone.

Do not issue endless moral clearance.

Do not dismiss stated intent, threats, planning, escalating violence, weapon access, or other concrete risk information as "just intrusive thoughts."

A safe partner response is:

"I know this question has been part of your OCD before. I don't want to keep deciding whether you're a good or dangerous person. If you are telling me you might act, have a plan, or cannot stay safe, we need professional help now."

This sets a clear distinction between a reassurance loop and actual risk disclosure.

Violence and Coercion Override the Plan

A person may become angry when accommodation is reduced.

Anger is not the same as violence.

A raised voice is not the same as being trapped in a room.

A complaint is not the same as a threat.

Your safety screen should flag:

physical violence,

threats of violence,

blocking exits,

destroying property to force compliance,

taking your phone or keys,

threatening children, pets, or other people,

coercive control,

stalking or monitoring,

threatening self-harm specifically to force a ritual from you.

If these are present, your priority is safety, not consistency with a workbook.

Seek help appropriate to your country and circumstances. That may include emergency services, domestic-abuse resources, legal advice, trusted people, or a safety-planning professional.

Do not announce a high-conflict accommodation change if doing so would put you at risk.

Dependent Safety Has Its Own Weight

Children, older adults, disabled dependents, and animals may be affected by OCD-driven rules or conflict.

A child required to wash repeatedly until skin is damaged is not merely participating in a household preference.

A dependent person denied necessary care because of contamination fear requires action.

A pet denied food, water, veterinary care, or safe access because of a ritual raises a real welfare problem.

Do not wait for the person with OCD to agree that the rule is unreasonable before protecting a dependent.

Professional guidance may be needed because legal responsibilities vary by place.

The safety screen asks, "Who else is carrying the consequence?"

Driving Requires Real Standards

Driving can attract checking and harm fears.

A driver may repeatedly retrace a route to see whether they hit someone. A partner may be asked to look backward, scan the road, or confirm every bump.

Those can become accommodation.

At the same time, driving has real safety rules.

If there is an actual collision, a warning, an observed hazard, or reasonable reason to think an incident occurred, follow traffic law and safety procedures.

If there is no new information and the request is another retracing ritual after an ordinary drive, that is a different pattern.

Do not encourage someone to continue driving if they are too distressed, impaired, sleepy, intoxicated, medicated in a way that affects driving, or otherwise unsafe. Real driving fitness is not an OCD exposure question for a partner to solve.

Appliances and Household Hazards Need an Ordinary Standard

A useful way to reduce uncertainty is to define the ordinary safety procedure outside the live moment.

For the stove: the person who cooked turns off the burners and performs one normal visual check.

For doors: the last person out locks the door once.

For candles: extinguish according to ordinary fire-safety practice.

For electrical equipment: follow manufacturer and workplace instructions.

Then decide what *does not* belong to the procedure.

Photographing the appliance five times.

Returning home after a completed check without new information.

Requiring the partner to certify the angle of every knob.

Repeatedly touching a lock.

The ordinary standard gives you a stable anchor.

The "New Information" Rule Needs Restraint

OCD is excellent at manufacturing something that *feels* new.

"What if I checked the wrong burner?"

"What if the sound I heard was different?"

"What if the photo has a shadow?"

Not every new sentence contains new information.

Define new information as a material external change: an alarm, smell, warning, observed event, message, professional instruction, or other fact that changes the risk assessment.

A new hypothetical is not automatically new information.

This is not a legal definition. It is a practical way to keep a safety exception from swallowing the boundary.

Make a Personal Safety and Escalation Plan

Write down the contacts and procedures you would use in a real crisis.

Do this before a crisis if possible.

Situation	My first action	Professional or emergency contact
Immediate medical danger	Follow emergency procedure	Local emergency service
Medication error or poisoning concern	Seek professional guidance	Pharmacist, prescriber, poison service
Credible self-harm risk	Stay with safety priorities, get help	Crisis or emergency service
Violence or threat	Move to safety if possible	Emergency or domestic-abuse support
Child/dependent safety concern	Protect dependent, seek advice	Appropriate professional or authority
Routine OCD reassurance loop	Use Support Pivot	Treatment plan if applicable

Fill in actual numbers and services for your country. Do not rely on a generic book during an emergency.

Keep the plan somewhere accessible.

Safety Does Not Require Zero Risk

One reason accommodation grows is that partners start using safety as a synonym for certainty.

No relationship can remove all risk.

Ordinary safety means using proportionate procedures, responding to credible information, and obtaining professional help where judgment exceeds your role.

It does not mean proving that nothing bad can happen.

That is the line OCD repeatedly tries to cross.

Your Support Pivot can therefore include safety:

"We did the ordinary safety step. There is no new information. I'm not doing another check."

If there *is* new information, act on it.

Write the Safety Exception Before You Need It

A boundary becomes easier to hold when the exception is already defined.

For a door-check target, write: "I will respond to an actual security alert, an observed open door, or a credible new report. I will not respond to a new hypothetical about a completed check."

For a health target: "I will act on new symptoms or the clinician's specified warning signs. I will not repeat the same inspection after the plan has been followed."

For driving: "We respond to an actual collision, warning, or observed hazard. We do not retrace the route only because a bump feels uncertain."

The examples are not universal safety rules. They show the form of a useful exception.

If you cannot write the exception without guessing, that is a sign to seek professional guidance first.

In a Nutshell

Do not use "it's OCD" as a reason to ignore real danger. Do not use intense anxiety as proof that a feared catastrophe is real.

Run the safety screen first: new objective information, recognized procedure, first response versus repetition, ordinary non-OCD standard, and need for professional judgment.

Medical emergencies, medication errors, credible self-harm risk, violence, coercion, and dependent safety override an accommodation plan.

Once ordinary safety is addressed, repeated certainty seeking can return to the Support Pivot.

Chapter 16 closes the practical arc by showing what recovery looks like from the partner's side, including progress that is easy to miss because anxiety and flare-ups still happen.

Chapter 16: Recovery From Your Side

Priya still asked Marcus for reassurance.

That fact would have disappointed him six months earlier.

What changed was everything around the question.

She sometimes caught herself and stopped. Marcus answered once and then returned to dinner. Laundry no longer required him to inspect her hands. Friends used the couch. A difficult evening did not automatically cancel the next day's plans. Priya had started treatment again. Marcus had restarted his Saturday football game.

OCD was still present.

It was no longer the organizing principle of the household.

From the partner's side, that is a meaningful recovery marker.

Do Not Use Zero Symptoms as the Only Score

OCD can have a fluctuating course, and treatment goals are not captured by a partner counting how many intrusive thoughts another person has. NICE notes that symptoms can recur and that treatment principles may need to be applied again if they do. (National Institute for Health and Care Excellence, 2005)

A partner often has access to different data.

How much reassurance are you providing?

How often are you checking for them?

How many house rules are fear-driven?

Can ordinary plans proceed?

Can both people tolerate an unfinished feeling without turning it into a couple project?

Is treatment work staying with the person and clinician rather than moving into the relationship?

Can you disagree without every disagreement becoming an OCD emergency?

These are **recovery markers** from your side.

They do not replace clinical measures. They tell you whether shared life is becoming larger.

Track Less Accommodation

The most direct marker is your own behavior.

You may still be asked the same question, but you answer once instead of eight times.

You may still hear a checking request, but you do not perform it.

You may still feel the urge to cancel a plan to avoid conflict, but you go.

The request surviving does not erase the change.

This matters because partners can become discouraged when symptoms remain visible. Family accommodation is only one part of OCD. Reducing your participation does not guarantee a particular symptom trajectory.

A 2024 meta-analysis found that accommodation decreased across individual and family-focused CBT, while baseline accommodation did not predict the amount of pre-to-post symptom change in the simple way one might expect. The relationship between accommodation and outcomes is important but not a one-variable story. (Hermida-Barros et al., 2024)

Your job is to keep your side clear.

Track More Responsibility

A second marker is responsibility returning to the person with OCD.

They make their own treatment appointments.

They use their own treatment plan.

They complete ordinary checks without asking you to certify them.

They make a decision without requiring you to guarantee the outcome.

They notice a reassurance urge and choose whether to ask.

They repair after a conflict rather than requiring you to prove it means nothing.

Responsibility does not mean isolation.

Partners still help each other.

The difference is that help is chosen for the person or practical task, not demanded as a condition for certainty.

Track More Flexibility

OCD-driven rules are often rigid.

Recovery may look like a rule becoming negotiable.

The route can change.

A visitor can sit down without a ritual.

Dinner can happen even if something feels unfinished.

A plan can proceed after a rough morning.

A thought can remain unclassified.

A partner can be unavailable for an hour.

The person with OCD may still feel distress. Flexibility means behavior is less dictated by it.

This is one reason ordinary-life restoration matters as much as symptom talk.

Track More Ordinary Life

At the beginning of this book, you mapped what disappeared.

Now track what returned.

Sleep.

Friends.

A shared room.

Sex that is not a test.

Travel.

Work concentration.

A hobby.

Dinner on time.

Children playing without ritual roles.

A conversation that has nothing to do with OCD.

These markers are concrete enough that you can notice them without monitoring your partner's internal state.

When one returns, protect it.

If you restarted a weekly class, do not automatically surrender it after the first relapse week.

Recovery that leaves the partner's life permanently suspended is incomplete from the relationship's perspective.

Expect Flare-Ups Without Resetting the Whole System

Stress, illness, transitions, grief, conflict, travel, sleep loss, and other changes can coincide with more symptoms.

The old request may come back.

A common partner reaction is either panic or surrender.

Panic says, "We're back at the beginning."

Surrender says, "Fine, I'll check until this passes."

Try maintenance instead.

Recognize the old pattern.

Use the established response.

Temporarily simplify by holding the most important accommodation limits rather than adding new ones.

Encourage the person to return to their treatment plan or professional support if they have one.

Protect safety.

Keep ordinary life moving where possible.

A flare-up is not proof that previous progress was fake.

Lapses on Your Side Need a Small Repair

You will reassure sometimes.

You will check.

You will cancel.

You will answer because you are tired and want sleep.

Do not turn one lapse into a week of accommodation.

Use a three-line reset.

"What did I do?"

"What made it easy to slip?"

"What will I do on the next request?"

Then continue.

If the lapse reveals that the target was unrealistic, adjust it deliberately rather than pretending the old rule still exists.

For example, maybe "no reassurance after 10 p.m." was too broad because genuine relationship conversations happen then. Refine it to "no repeat certainty questions after the first answer."

Precision beats guilt.

Review the Support Pivot

At this point, the Support Pivot should be shorter in practice than it looked on paper.

Notice the pattern.

Meet the person.

Decline the accommodation.

Return the next choice.

For a familiar request, that can be one sentence.

"I know the doubt is back. I'm not checking again. Let's keep packing."

For relationship certainty:

"I know you want another answer. I meant what I said, and I'm not repeating the test."

For a household rule:

"I know this feels contaminated. Guests can use the couch normally."

For treatment:

"I'll support the appointment. I won't monitor your homework."

For safety:

"There is new information, so we're following the real safety procedure."

The framework is not meant to make you sound scripted forever. It is meant to train discrimination until your own response becomes ordinary.

Let Treatment Progress Belong to Your Partner

One of the strangest outcomes of heavy accommodation is that the partner becomes as invested in symptom metrics as the person with OCD.

You watch whether anxiety dropped.

You ask whether exposure happened.

You notice ritual time.

You monitor whether reassurance was sought elsewhere.

That attention may have grown from care.

Recovery requires giving some of it back.

If your partner wants to share progress, listen.

If a clinician asks for specific observations with consent, provide them.

Otherwise, do not make the relationship into a surveillance system.

Your recovery marker is not "I know everything about the OCD."

It is "I no longer have to know everything in order to live my part of the relationship."

The Thirty-Day Steady Support Plan

Use the next thirty days to move from active change into maintenance.

Choose three accommodation limits you will keep.

Choose two ordinary-life commitments you will protect.

Choose one household rule you will not reinstate during a bad week.

Choose one treatment-role boundary.

Choose one safety plan you have written down.

Choose a date to review, rather than reviewing every night.

Your plan might look like this:

Area	Thirty-day commitment
Reassurance	One ordinary answer, no repeated certainty answers
Checking	No delegated stove or door checks
Household	Visitors use shared furniture normally
Ordinary life	Saturday sport and Wednesday dinner with friend
Treatment role	Attend session if invited, no homework policing
Safety	Use written crisis and medical contacts
Review	First Sunday next month

The plan should be boring.

Boring is good.

It means the relationship is no longer inventing policy in the middle of every episode.

Know When the Relationship Needs a Bigger Decision

Reducing accommodation can clarify a relationship, but it cannot solve every relationship.

You may reach a point where the remaining problem is not "How do I answer reassurance?"

It may be:

Can I stay if my partner refuses treatment and the household remains restricted?

Can we parent safely together?

Can I accept the level of impairment that remains?

Can we repair trust after years of conflict?

Is there coercion or abuse?

Do we want the same kind of life?

Those questions are not failures of the method.

They are adult relationship questions.

Seek appropriate support. A couples therapist can help with relationship decisions where safe and suitable. Individual support can help you make decisions without requiring your partner to agree first. Legal or financial advice may be necessary for separation, housing, or custody questions.

The purpose of this book is not to keep every relationship together.

It is to help you make choices with clearer boundaries around OCD.

What Support Looks Like Now

At the beginning, support may have meant making distress stop.

By the end, support can look different.

You can listen without solving.

You can care without certifying.

You can help with treatment logistics without becoming the therapist.

You can keep a real safety procedure without repeating it for certainty.

You can allow your partner to be upset with a boundary.

You can protect children and your own life.

You can enjoy good hours without asking whether they mean recovery is complete.

The relationship becomes less organized around a single question: "How do we make this feeling go away?"

It gains other questions.

"What do we want for dinner?"

"Who are we seeing this weekend?"

"What do you think about that film?"

"Do we still want to move?"

"What are you working on?"

"What do I want?"

Ordinary questions are not trivial. They are evidence that the household has subjects other than OCD.

Let Boring Be a Recovery Marker

Couples can become so accustomed to intensity that an ordinary evening feels suspicious.

Nobody asks the door question.

Dinner happens.

One person reads.

The other answers a message.

There is no big conversation about progress.

You may be tempted to point it out.

"See how good tonight was?"

Sometimes that is welcome. Sometimes it turns ordinary life back into symptom observation.

Let some good hours pass without commentary.

This is especially important for the partner who has become the household monitor. You do not have to convert every quiet evening into evidence that the plan is working.

The larger life you are trying to restore contains many moments that are not memorable.

They are not supposed to be.

A relationship should have enough room for boredom, errands, unfinished conversations, bad television, separate hobbies, ordinary affection, and plans that do not teach anyone a lesson.

When those moments return, participate in them rather than grading them.

Keep a Maintenance Note, Not a Dossier

You may want a record for future flare-ups. Keep it to one page.

Write the three accommodation limits that matter most, the two safety exceptions you have clarified, the clinician or service to contact if treatment needs to restart, and the ordinary-life commitments you want to protect.

Do not keep a detailed archive of every symptom unless a clinician has asked for it.

A short maintenance note helps memory without turning your partner into a case file.

Review it at a planned interval or when a meaningful change occurs.

Then close it.

The goal is to know your response well enough that you can spend less time preparing for OCD and more time living around subjects that have nothing to do with it.

In a Nutshell

From the partner's side, recovery is visible in less accommodation, more responsibility, more flexibility, and more ordinary life.

Expect flare-ups. Hold established limits. Reset lapses without drama. Keep treatment ownership where it belongs.

Use the Thirty-Day Steady Support Plan to make the new responses predictable enough that they stop feeling like a daily campaign.

The last task is to decide what kind of life all this boundary work was meant to make room for.

Conclusion: Make Room for a Larger Life

The first accommodation you change may feel tiny.

One answer you do not repeat.

One check you stop doing.

One chair visitors can use.

One evening you do not spend proving a fear false.

One class you attend even though your partner is distressed.

Small changes matter here because accommodation grows the same way: one reasonable exception, one urgent request, one peaceful workaround at a time.

The point was never to become a partner who says no more often.

The point was to become a partner whose yes and no are no longer organized primarily around OCD.

Keep the Central Distinction

You can support the person without doing the compulsion's job.

That distinction has carried every chapter.

Support can be affection, practical help, listening, shared responsibility, treatment logistics, ordinary reassurance, safety action, humor, sex, repair, patience, distance, or a firm limit.

Accommodation is narrower. It is the part of your behavior that repeatedly provides certainty, completes checking, participates in ritual, facilitates avoidance, or reorganizes routine in response to OCD.

The two can feel similar in the moment because both may reduce distress.

That is why you learned to look at function.

What happens after the answer?

Can the information stand?

Who owns the responsibility?

Is the household becoming more flexible or less?

What ordinary life is being displaced?

These questions are more useful than trying to become perfectly certain about whether a request is "really OCD."

Keep the Support Pivot Small

Notice the pattern.

Meet the person.

Decline the accommodation.

Return the next choice.

You do not have to say all four steps.

The mature version of the Support Pivot may sound like:

"I know this is hard. I already answered."

"I'm here. I'm not checking."

"We'll follow the actual safety plan. I won't add another certainty check."

"We can talk about the real relationship problem tomorrow. I won't keep testing whether we are okay tonight."

The method should eventually disappear into ordinary speech.

If you sound like a textbook during every argument, simplify.

Make Graded Reduction a Habit

Do not finish this book by declaring a household revolution.

Look at your Accommodation Map.

Choose the next target.

Pair it with one restoration target.

Tell your partner what you are changing when it is safe and useful to do so.

Hold the response long enough to learn.

Review.

Then move.

The process is deliberately slower than resentment wants and faster than indefinite waiting.

You do not need to eliminate every accommodation. Some are unclear. Some may be part of legitimate care. Some may be embedded in a clinician's plan. Some may be low-cost compromises you consciously choose to keep.

The goal is not purity.

It is choice.

Protect the Relationship From Becoming a Treatment Program

If your partner is in treatment, let the clinician direct treatment.

If your partner refuses treatment, do not become the replacement clinician.

If a family session gives you a specific role, write it down.

If you do not have a role, stay with your behavior.

If a real relationship issue appears, treat it as a relationship issue.

If a safety issue appears, treat it as safety.

These distinctions protect both people from the assumption that OCD explains everything.

A relationship can contain OCD and still contain incompatibility, joy, unfairness, desire, boredom, money trouble, parenting questions, illness, private interests, friendship, grief, humor, and change.

Leave room for the whole relationship.

Let Your Own Life Become Visible Again

You may have started this book because your partner asks too much of you.

You may finish it noticing how much you stopped asking of your own life.

What do you want your week to contain?

Who do you want to see?

What do you want to protect in your work?

How much sleep do you need?

What kind of parent, friend, sibling, worker, lover, or private person do you want to be?

Those are not rewards you receive after OCD improves.

They are part of the environment in which both people are adults.

Restoring your own life can feel selfish when constant availability has become normal. Use a more accurate standard: is the life you are building fair, safe, sustainable, and compatible with the responsibilities you genuinely choose?

If yes, keep building it.

Recovery Does Not Need a Perfect Ending

The relationship may improve.

Treatment may work well.

Accommodation may fall dramatically.

Some symptoms may remain.

Treatment may be interrupted.

Your partner may refuse help.

You may decide to live separately.

You may stay and build stronger boundaries.

You may discover that the relationship problem is larger than OCD.

A self-help book should not promise which ending is yours.

It can give you a better position from which to make decisions.

You can know what family accommodation is.

You can recognize the reassurance loop.

You can stop solving content.

You can hand back checking.

You can reclaim shared space.

You can set a limit without making yourself the therapist.

You can protect children and your own life.

You can distinguish ordinary safety from compulsive certainty.

That is enough structure to change the part of the system that belongs to you.

Your Next Thirty Days

Do not create a long plan tonight.

Write five lines.

One accommodation I will reduce:

One ordinary-life activity I will restore:

One sentence I will use when the request repeats:

One safety or treatment question that belongs with a professional:

One date when I will review instead of judging the plan every day:

Put the page somewhere you can find it.

Then return to your life.

The strongest sign that OCD has less authority may not be a dramatic breakthrough. It may be that an evening passes and neither of you spends it discussing certainty.

The question comes.

You know what it is asking you to do.

You answer the person, not the compulsion.

And the rest of the evening remains available.

Appendices:

Appendix A: Accommodation Audit and Household Map

This appendix turns the book's ideas into a repeatable audit. Use it when you first identify accommodation, after a flare-up, when a new symptom theme begins affecting shared life, or every few months if the household changes gradually.

The purpose is not to measure how "good" or "bad" either partner is. It is to identify behaviors the non-OCD partner performs and decide which ones are reasonable candidates for change.

Step One: Record What You Actually Do

For seven days, record accommodations as they happen. Use verbs.

Do not write "OCD ruins mornings." Write "I answer the locked-door question four to six times and then photograph the handle."

Do not write "We avoid germs." Write "I ask visitors to wash twice and place their bags in a separate area."

Do not write "They make me manage everything." Write "I open the banking app after every transfer and confirm the recipient, amount, and balance."

Concrete descriptions let you choose concrete limits.

Date	What I did	What came immediately before	What happened right after

If you do the same action many times, use one line and record frequency.

Example: "Answered relationship certainty question approximately 12 times between 9 and 11 p.m."

Approximate counts are enough for planning. Do not spend more time measuring accommodation than you used to spend doing it.

Step Two: Classify by Function

Use the five accommodation types from Chapter 2.

Reassurance: repeated certainty, memory confirmation, safety guarantees, moral clearance, relationship proof, probability estimates.

Participation: joining a ritual, repeating a phrase, washing, arranging, counting, confessing, or completing part of a compulsion.

Delegated checking: performing, witnessing, photographing, recording, or certifying a check so responsibility transfers to you.

Facilitated avoidance: canceling, rerouting, removing, researching alternatives, making excuses, or taking over a task to prevent contact with a feared situation.

Routine modification: reorganizing household space, time, visitors, meals, sleep, travel, parenting, finances, or intimacy around OCD-related distress.

One behavior can have more than one function. Choose the closest match.

Behavior	Reassurance	Participatio n	Delegated checking	Facilitated avoidance	Routine modification

The categories exist to clarify the pattern, not to force a perfect label.

Step Three: Run the Function Test

For each candidate accommodation, answer these questions.

Does it repeat? A one-time practical help can be ordinary. Repetition after the problem is already addressed is more suggestive of accommodation.

Is the goal information or certainty? Information can be incomplete and still useful. Certainty demands tend to escalate.

Does the action transfer responsibility? Are you becoming responsible for the check, memory, prediction, moral conclusion, health interpretation, or relationship guarantee?

Does relief last? Short relief followed by the same request is a strong pattern marker.

Does the standard expand? One wash becomes two. One answer needs a different wording. One photograph needs a closer angle.

Would you choose the same behavior if OCD-related distress were not present? A yes may indicate a normal preference or legitimate responsibility.

Is there a safety, medical, disability, cultural, religious, legal, work, or parenting reason for the behavior? If yes or unclear, pause before labeling it an accommodation.

Use the table to summarize.

Behavior	Repeats	Seeks certainty	Transfers responsibility	Short relief	Expands	Legitimate reason unclear

A row with several "yes" answers is a stronger accommodation candidate. A safety or legitimate-reason flag means "clarify first," not "push harder."

Step Four: Map the OCD Footprint

Now move from individual behaviors to domains.

Time

Record time spent answering, checking, waiting, repeating, researching, washing, driving, or recovering from accommodation conflict.

Ask what the time replaced.

Did you miss sleep, work, meals, school departure, exercise, friendship, sex, leisure, or rest?

Space

List restricted or special areas.

Rooms, chairs, beds, bathrooms, shelves, counters, cars, routes, entrances, "clean" zones, "dirty" zones, places children cannot go.

Ask whether the rule is flexible and whether shared household members consented to it.

Work and Money

List direct costs.

Replacement items, transport, cancellation charges, repeated professional consultations, cleaning products, missed work, reduced hours, lost opportunities, or purchases made to satisfy a certainty rule.

Do not assume every treatment or medical cost is accommodation. Professional care can be appropriate. The question is whether the spending itself is part of repeated certainty seeking or avoidance.

Sleep

Record delayed bedtime, waking, separate sleeping arrangements, alarms, repeated checks, reassurance after lights out, and your own sleep loss.

Sleep is often a high-value restoration target because it affects every other limit.

Social Life

List invitations declined, visitors restricted, restaurants avoided, travel canceled, family events changed, or friends recruited into reassurance.

Ask which social choices you want back.

Intimacy and Family

List touch rules, sexual avoidance, confession loops, relationship testing, child participation, relative involvement, or caregiving tasks taken over.

Do not use this map to pressure sexual activity. Consent remains separate from accommodation.

Domain	What OCD-related accommodation changes	Cost to me or household	Ordinary choice I want back
Time			
Space			
Work and money			
Sleep			
Social life			
Intimacy and family			

Step Five: Identify Hidden Adaptations

Complete these sentences.

"I stopped mentioning ______ because I expect a reassurance loop."

"I automatically check ______ before my partner asks."

"I avoid inviting ______ because of the rules around ______."

"I stay available during ______ because I expect a call or question."

"I handle ______ now even though it used to be shared."

"I no longer do ______ because the conflict feels too expensive."

Hidden adaptations are strong candidates for restoration because they may be under your control without requiring a direct confrontation.

Step Six: Rank Change Difficulty

Mark each behavior L, M, H, or C.

L, low difficulty: specific, frequent, low genuine safety stakes, little effect on dependents, easy to define.

M, medium difficulty: affects a shared routine, more distress or conflict likely, may need advance agreement.

H, high difficulty: affects children, housing, sex, substantial money, severe avoidance, long-standing rituals, or intense conflict. Consider professional support.

C, clarify first: possible medical, safety, legal, disability, occupational, cultural, religious, or other legitimate reason.

Accommodation	Level	Why	What would make it safer or clearer to change?

Choose one L item first unless a more urgent dependent-safety or relationship issue requires professional action.

Step Seven: Pair Reduction With Restoration

For every accommodation target, name what you want to regain.

Accommodation target	Restoration target
Stop repeated door reassurance	Leave home on time
Stop photographing appliances	Put phone away after departure
Stop visitor washing rule	Host a normal meal
Stop after-midnight relationship tests	Sleep
Stop delegated email review	Have work-free evenings
Stop canceling class	Attend weekly activity

Write your own pair.

I will reduce: ______________________________________

So that I can restore: ________________________________

The second line is the reason to keep the first.

Step Eight: Check Whose Job It Is

Before changing a behavior, sort responsibility.

My job: my speech, my checking, my time, my phone, my participation, my personal plans, my side of shared agreements.

Shared job: household money, children, housing, jointly owned property, agreed safety procedures, shared schedules.

My partner's job: their treatment decisions, their private rituals, their homework, their internal certainty, their decision whether to seek care.

Professional job: diagnosis, clinical treatment design, medication, crisis assessment, specialized risk or legal judgment.

Accommodation grows when these categories blur.

Use the table.

Issue	My job	Shared job	Partner's job	Professional job
Repeated reassurance	My response		Ask or not ask	Treatment guidance if needed
Shared budget		Yes		Financial/legal advice if needed
ERP homework			Primary responsibility	Clinician directs
Medication change			Patient decision with prescriber	Prescriber

Issue	My job	Shared job	Partner's job	Professional job
Child ritual role	My boundary	Co-parenting		Family/child professional if needed

Step Nine: Write the First Partner Limit

Use this formula:

"I will / will not ______ when ______. If ______, I will ______."

Examples:

"I will answer a normal first question once. If the same certainty question repeats, I will say I already answered and return to what I was doing."

"I will not photograph the stove after we leave. If there is genuinely new safety information, we will follow the ordinary safety procedure."

"I will not ask the children to reassure either parent. If an adult question is directed at them repeatedly, I will step in."

"I will protect sleep after eleven. If there is a real emergency, we use the safety plan."

Avoid vague phrases such as "I will set better boundaries." A useful limit can be observed.

Step Ten: Review Without Prosecution

At the review date, answer five questions.

What did I do consistently?

Where did I get pulled into debate?

What ordinary life returned?

What safety or legitimate-care issue did I discover?

What is the next smallest change?

Do not ask, "Did my partner get better because I did this?"

That conclusion requires more evidence than a household week can provide.

Your audit is about your participation.

Keep the completed map. A later comparison can show progress that memory misses.

Appendix B: Support Pivot Script Bank

Scripts are useful when you already know the behavior you are changing. They are not a substitute for deciding whether a request is ordinary, compulsive, or safety-related.

Use the shortest sentence that fits. Say it in your normal voice. If a script sounds like something you would never say, rewrite it.

The categories below give options for common partner situations.

Repeated Reassurance

First repeat after an ordinary answer:

"I already gave you my answer. I don't want to keep trying to make it feel certain."

"I know you want me to say it again. I'm going to leave my first answer where it is."

"I've told you what I know. I don't have more certainty to add."

"This feels like the same question coming back. I'm not going to answer it again."

If the question changes wording but not function:

"I hear the new wording. I think it is asking me for the same certainty."

"That detail does not change what I'm doing. I won't reopen the answer."

"We can deal with genuinely new information. I won't keep testing the same fear."

If you are getting drawn into explanation:

"I'm starting to argue the case again. I'm stopping here."

"I don't want to spend the evening proving this."

"I've moved from answering to investigating. I'm done with the investigation."

If you want to offer presence:

"I'm not going to answer the question again. I can sit with you for a few minutes."

"I won't give another certainty answer. We can keep walking."

"I know this is rough. I'm staying with the plan."

Moral, Harm, and Guilt Reassurance

When asked to certify character:

"I care about you, and I don't want to keep issuing a verdict on what the thought means."

"I know the thought is upsetting. I won't keep deciding whether it proves something about you."

"I'm not going to answer the good-person or bad-person test."

When asked to interpret an intrusive thought:

"I don't want to keep analyzing what the thought means."

"That sounds like another request for certainty about the thought. I'm stepping out of the analysis."

"If you need help deciding how to respond to intrusive thoughts, that belongs in treatment rather than in repeated reassurance from me."

When there is actual risk language:

"If you are telling me you might act, have a plan, or cannot stay safe, we need professional help now. If this is the same reassurance question, I won't keep answering it."

Do not use that sentence mechanically if you have real reason to believe there is danger. In that case, act on safety.

Health Reassurance

After an appropriate medical step has already occurred:

"We followed the medical advice for this. I won't keep inspecting the same symptom."

"If the situation changes in the way the clinician told us to watch for, we'll act. I won't recheck it every ten minutes."

"I don't know how to guarantee that nothing is wrong. We have an appropriate medical plan."

When asked to search online:

"I won't search for another explanation. If we need medical advice, let's use a proper medical channel."

"I don't want to compare more photos or symptom lists."

When there is genuinely new information:

"That is new information. Let's treat it as a real medical question rather than an OCD exercise."

Delegated Checking

Door or appliance:

"The ordinary check is done. I won't do another one."

"I'm not going back to photograph it."

"I won't certify the handle after you've checked."

"Whoever closes it does the normal check once. I'm not adding a second layer."

Digital checking:

"I won't reopen the app to prove the transfer again."

"I'm not rereading the sent message."

"We keep location sharing for ordinary convenience. I won't answer repeated questions about the map."

"I gave feedback before you sent it. I'm not reviewing it after the fact for certainty."

Witnessing:

"I won't stand there to confirm that you checked."

"I trust you to handle the ordinary task. I won't be the witness."

"I won't tell you whether the check looked exact enough."

Contamination and Washing Requests

Extra washing:

"I used the ordinary hygiene step. I won't wash again for certainty."

"I know you want another wash. I'm not doing it."

"I won't ask the kids or visitors to wash again."

Surface rules:

"I'll use the shared counter normally."

"I won't move that object into the special area."

"Guests can sit on the furniture."

"I won't clean the chair because someone used it."

If there is a real infection-control reason:

"This is a genuine health situation, so we'll follow the relevant medical or public-health guidance. We won't add extra rules beyond that without a reason."

Avoidance Requests

Canceled plans:

"I know you would rather avoid it. I'm keeping my plan."

"I won't cancel the visit because of this fear."

"You can decide whether you come. I'm still going."

Route changes:

"I'm taking the ordinary route we planned."

"I won't drive extra miles to make the uncertainty disappear."

"If there is an actual road hazard, we'll change route. The fear by itself is not changing the plan."

Tasks taken over:

"I won't do that task only so you can avoid the trigger."

"I can help with the normal workload. I won't take over this part as an OCD workaround."

Household Rules

Shared space:

"I want this room to be shared space. I won't enforce that OCD rule here."

"I'll respect your personal drawer. I won't organize my things by the same rule."

"The family will use the kitchen according to our ordinary standard."

Visitors:

"I won't give visitors ritual instructions."

"They do not need to answer the same question."

"I won't ask your family to participate in the checking."

Children:

"The kids are not responsible for reassurance."

"I'll handle the adult disagreement. The child is not doing the ritual."

"You can ask me about the house rule. Do not ask the kids to certify it."

Relationship Reassurance

Repeated love question:

"I've answered you honestly. I don't want love to become a test I have to keep passing."

"I want to say I love you because I mean it, not because the phrase has to remove every doubt."

"I know this uncertainty hurts. I won't keep proving the relationship."

Compatibility:

"We can talk about actual problems we want to solve. I won't decide whether we're perfectly compatible."

"We do not need a final verdict on the whole relationship tonight."

"I can tell you what I want now. I cannot promise the entire future."

Attraction:

"I won't rank you against other people."

"I'll honor our relationship agreements. I won't report every attraction or glance."

"I don't want our intimacy to become a checking system."

Confession:

"If information affects our agreements, I need honesty. I don't need every intrusive thought reported for clearance."

"I won't decide whether each thought needs a confession."

"If you are unsure whether telling me is compulsive, take that question to treatment."

After a real conflict:

"We do need to repair what happened. I won't answer whether the argument proves we're wrong for each other."

"I'm willing to discuss what I said and what I will change. I won't guarantee what the conflict means about our future."

"We can schedule the relationship conversation. I'm not doing the certainty loop tonight."

Treatment Discussions

When invited to help:

"Tell me the exact role your clinician wants me to play."

"I'm willing to change this accommodation. I don't want to design exposures."

"I can attend a session if you want. I won't monitor treatment all day."

When asked to judge homework:

"I don't want to grade whether you did treatment correctly."

"That sounds like a question for your therapist."

"I'll encourage you if you ask. I won't certify the exposure."

Medication:

"I can help you contact the prescriber. I won't tell you how to change the dose."

"I don't know whether that side effect is clinically important. Let's ask the appropriate professional."

"Please do not stop or change prescribed medication based on my guess."

Treatment Refusal

Opening the conversation:

"The OCD-related routines are taking a lot of our shared life. I think we need specialist help."

"I would like you to get an assessment from someone experienced with OCD. I can help with logistics if you want."

"You get to decide whether you seek treatment. I still get to decide what rituals I participate in."

When persuasion repeats:

"I've told you why I hope you'll get help. I don't want to argue about it every night."

"My invitation stands. I'm not going to keep selling therapy to you."

"I can't be the replacement clinician. I can be your partner."

When refusal affects your limit:

"Treatment is your decision. My sleep boundary is still my decision."

"You do not have to agree with my view of accommodation. I am still not doing the repeated check."

Anger and Conflict

When accused of cruelty:

"I hear that this feels rejecting. I don't want to reject you. I still won't do the check."

"We can talk later about how I set the limit. I'm not reopening the fear right now."

"If my tone was harsh, I will own that. The boundary still stands."

When the conversation keeps circling:

"We are repeating the argument. I'm going to stop talking about this topic."

"I can talk about something else. I won't keep defending the limit."

"We'll review the plan tomorrow at six, not in the middle of this request."

Exit:

"I'm going to another room for twenty minutes. I won't continue this topic when I come back."

"I need sleep. Unless there is a real emergency, I'm done with reassurance questions tonight."

"I am ending this conversation because we are no longer speaking respectfully."

If leaving is blocked or you are afraid, move from a communication strategy to a safety strategy.

Family and Friends

To a relative who wants to help:

"We're reducing repeated reassurance. Please answer ordinary questions normally, but do not keep giving the same certainty."

"You don't need to become part of the treatment. Just keep the visit ordinary."

"Please do not ask the children to check."

To a child:

"You do not have to answer that again."

"Grown-ups will handle it."

"You are not responsible for making anyone feel certain."

"You can come to me if a rule feels confusing or scary."

To a friend without diagnostic disclosure:

"You already answered the question. You don't need to keep proving it."

"No special cleaning is needed in our home."

"We'll handle that ourselves."

Protecting Your Time

Work:

"I'm not available for nonurgent reassurance while I'm in meetings."

"I'll check messages at lunch. If there is a real emergency, tell me what happened."

Sleep:

"I'm not doing repeated OCD questions after eleven."

"If something genuinely new and urgent happens, wake me. Otherwise, we'll talk tomorrow."

Personal plans:

"I'm going to my class. I won't cancel because the uncertainty is high."

"I'll be home at the time we planned. I won't stay on the phone doing reassurance while I'm out."

Privacy:

"I'll share information that affects our agreements. I won't provide a complete log of my thoughts or interactions."

"I'm not going to prove my location repeatedly."

Safety

Possible emergency:

"This is new information. We're following the real safety procedure."

"I don't know enough to judge this. We need professional advice."

"This is beyond a reassurance question. I'm getting help."

No new information after an ordinary safety step:

"We completed the normal safety check. I won't repeat it."

"If something materially changes, we'll act. A new hypothetical is not a new event."

Threats or violence:

"I am not going to negotiate safety in this moment."

"I am leaving now because I do not feel safe."

Use whatever language is safest. In real danger, the goal is not a polished script. It is safety.

How to Write Your Own Script

Use four elements.

Observation: "This is the same question again."

Human response: "I know the uncertainty is hard."

Limit: "I won't answer it again."

Next choice: "I'm going back to dinner."

Then compress.

Full: "This is the same question again. I know the uncertainty is hard. I won't answer it again. I'm going back to dinner."

Short: "I know. Same answer. I'm going back to dinner."

Repeat: "No change."

Your own words will usually work better than mine.

Write five custom scripts now.

Situation	Full response	Short response	Repeat response

The Script Quality Check

Before using a script, ask:

Does it describe my behavior rather than command theirs?

Does it avoid guaranteeing safety, morality, memory, or the future?

Does it leave genuine safety routes open?

Does it sound like a partner rather than a clinician?

Can I say it without a lecture?

Can I keep the same limit if my partner dislikes it?

If yes, the script is ready enough.

No sentence will make every moment easy. The script is there to keep you from inventing a new policy while under pressure.

Appendix C: Four-Week Accommodation Reduction Planner

This planner turns one accommodation target into a month of deliberate practice. It is not a clinical ERP hierarchy. It tracks the non-OCD partner's behavior and the return of ordinary life.

If your partner has a clinician-directed plan, use that plan instead of conflicting with it.

Before Week One

Choose one low-difficulty target from Appendix A.

Write it behaviorally.

Poor definition: "Stop enabling."

Better definition: "After I answer the locked-door question once, I will not answer another version of it during the same departure."

Poor definition: "Stop contamination accommodation."

Better definition: "I will use the shared couch normally and will not cover it for visitors."

Poor definition: "Stop checking."

Better definition: "I will not photograph the stove after the ordinary departure check."

Now pair it with a restoration target.

"I want us to leave on time."

"I want guests to use the living room normally."

"I want my phone to stay in my bag after we leave."

"I want to sleep after eleven."

"I want to attend my Thursday class."

Write your first pair.

Accommodation I will reduce: ______________________________

Ordinary life I want to restore: ______________________________

Confirm the Ordinary Standard

Before reducing a safety-related behavior, define the ordinary real-world procedure.

Example: "The last person out locks the door once."

Example: "The person who cooks turns off the appliance and performs one normal visual check."

Example: "We follow the clinician's medication instructions. Dose uncertainty goes to a pharmacist or prescriber."

Example: "We use normal hand hygiene for food preparation."

If you cannot define the ordinary standard because the question is medical, legal, occupational, or otherwise specialized, clarify it first.

Ordinary standard for this target: ______________________________

What would count as genuinely new information: ______________________________

Who can clarify if I am unsure: ______________________________

Announce the Change

Write a calm-period version of your plan.

Use three parts.

What I noticed: "I have noticed that..."

What I am changing: "From now on, I will..."

What remains: "I can still..."

Example:

"I've noticed that I reopen the banking app several times after we pay a bill. From now on, I'll review the payment once before it is sent and I won't reopen it for repeated certainty checks. I can still handle the banking tasks we agreed are mine and deal with a real bank alert if one appears."

Your version:

I noticed: ______________________________

I am changing: ______________________________

I can still: ______________________________

If advance discussion is unsafe because of threats or violence, do not use this worksheet as a confrontation plan. Use appropriate safety support.

Week One: Make the Target Visible

The first week is about consistency, not expansion.

Use the same limit.

Avoid adding a second target.

Track only your behavior.

Day	Target happened	I accommodated	I used the planned response	I debated after the limit	What ordinary life continued
Monday					
Tuesday					
Wednesday					
Thursday					
Friday					
Saturday					
Sunday					

At the end of the week, answer:

Where did I hold the limit most easily?

Where did I add too much explanation?

What time of day or condition made a lapse more likely?

Did I discover a real safety or legitimate-care issue I had overlooked?

What did I get back, even briefly?

Do not answer, "Was my partner less anxious?" That is not the measure here.

Week Two: Reduce the Debate

Keep Target A exactly the same.

Your new focus is what happens *after* the limit.

A partner can refuse a check and still spend twenty minutes justifying the refusal. The ritual changes shape but keeps the evening.

Choose a maximum number of explanations.

A useful rule is one explanation outside the live moment, one short response during it, then no new reasons.

Write your full response:

____

Write your short response:

____

Write your repeat response: ______________________________

Write your exit from the topic: ______________________________

Track the debate.

Day	Held Target A	Number of extra explanations	Used exit script	Returned to ordinary activity
Monday				
Tuesday				
Wednesday				
Thursday				
Friday				
Saturday				
Sunday				

End-of-week questions:
Which explanation tends to reopen the content?
Which sentence sounds most like me?
Can I tolerate being misunderstood without producing one more defense?
Am I using withdrawal or contempt instead of a clear limit?
Do I need a repair conversation about tone or respect?

Week Three: Add One New Target

Only add Target B if Target A is clear enough that you know what you will do.

Target B should usually be another low or medium-low difficulty behavior.

Target B: ______________________________

Restoration target B: ______________________________

Ordinary standard or safety exception: ______________________________

Full response: ______________________________

Short response: ______________________________

Keep Target A in maintenance.

Day	Target A held	Target B occurred	Target B held	What ordinary life continued
Monday				
Tuesday				
Wednesday				
Thursday				
Friday				
Saturday				
Sunday				

If both targets collapse because the plan has become too demanding, remove Target B for a week. That is adjustment, not defeat.

Week Four: Expand Ordinary Life

Keep the accommodation targets stable.

Use the final week to do something that the old pattern had displaced.

Choose one specific restoration action.

Examples:

Have two friends over without ritual instructions.

Go to a class and remain unavailable for nonurgent reassurance.

Take the ordinary route.

Eat dinner at the planned time.

Use a shared room normally.

Sleep in your own bed.

Let the children attend an activity without an OCD-driven rule.

Do not choose an action solely because it will trigger your partner. It should be something you genuinely value or an ordinary household function you want back.

My Week Four restoration action: ______________________________

Date and time: ______________________________

What accommodation I will not reinstate to make it easier: ______________

Real safety or practical plan, if any: ______________________________

Afterward, record what *you* did. ______________________________

The Month-End Review

Review the month as a whole.

Target A

Did I define it clearly?
Did I keep the ordinary safety standard?
How often did I hold it?
What situations pulled me back into accommodation?
What debate pattern followed?
What restoration happened?

Target B

Was it well chosen?
Did it interfere with Target A?
Do I keep, pause, narrow, or expand it?

Ordinary Life

What returned?
What remains absent?
Which restoration gave the biggest improvement in my own functioning?

Treatment Role

Did I become a homework monitor, exposure designer, or diagnosis referee?
If yes, what will I hand back?

Safety

Did any threat, medical issue, child concern, or coercive behavior appear?
If yes, what professional support is needed?

Relationship

Did I separate real relationship problems from OCD certainty loops?

What needs a genuine relationship conversation?

Decide the Next Month

Choose one of four paths.

Maintain: Keep the two targets and make no new changes for another month.

Expand: Add one new accommodation target.

Clarify: Pause new changes while you get professional advice about safety, treatment, parenting, medical, legal, or relationship questions.

Protect: Focus on your own safety, children, finances, sleep, housing, or support rather than further accommodation reduction.

Write your choice.

Next month's path: ____

Reason: ____

Review date: ____

A Filled Example

Marcus chooses repeated contamination reassurance.

Accommodation target: "I will answer an ordinary practical question about whether I washed once. I will not repeat the answer or demonstrate my hands."

Restoration target: "We will finish dinner without a twenty-minute hand-washing debate."

Ordinary standard: "Wash hands once at appropriate hygiene times, using ordinary household practice."

Week One: Marcus holds the limit four of six times. On two evenings he gives in after long arguments.

Week Two: He notices that his explanation, "Reassurance makes OCD worse," starts a debate about research. He replaces it with, "I answered once. I'm not doing another check."

Week Three: He adds a second target: no inspection of Priya's laundry sequence.

Week Four: They have his sister for dinner without asking her to follow the extra washing rule. Priya is distressed and leaves the table for part of the meal.

Marcus does not treat that as failure. The guest is not recruited into the ritual, and the evening continues.

Month-end decision: Maintain both targets another month before adding anything else.

The example is not a prediction. It shows the kind of data this planner values: clear partner behavior, visible ordinary life, and safety kept separate from certainty.

Keep the Planner in Proportion

If completing these tables starts consuming your attention, stop tracking.

The point is to reduce the amount of life organized around OCD.

A planner that becomes another nightly ritual is defeating its purpose.

Use it to decide, practice, and review.

Then put it away.

Appendix D: Partner Session and Treatment Conversation Worksheet

This appendix helps you prepare for a treatment conversation without taking over the treatment itself. Use it if your partner is considering OCD care, entering care, or inviting you into a session.

The worksheet has two rules.

First, record what you observe, not what you think your partner "really" believes.

Second, ask the clinician to define your role rather than volunteering for every task.

Before the Conversation

Write three concrete effects of OCD-related accommodation on shared life.

Avoid global statements.

Instead of "Everything is about OCD," write "We spend thirty to forty minutes most nights on repeated relationship questions."

Instead of "The house is impossible," write "Visitors are currently asked to wash twice and can use only one chair."

Instead of "I do all the work," write "I now perform the final checks for the stove, doors, and bank transfers."

Effect 1: ______________________________

Effect 2: ______________________________

Effect 3: ______________________________

Now write one thing you want treatment to help *you stop doing*.

____

This keeps your request focused on accommodation rather than on controlling every symptom.

If Your Partner Is Considering Treatment

You can help prepare questions without interviewing the clinician yourself unless your partner wants that.

Questions a prospective OCD clinician can answer include:
How do you assess OCD and distinguish it from related conditions?
Do you regularly treat adults with OCD?
What psychological approaches do you use for OCD?
How do you use exposure and response prevention when appropriate?
How do you address reassurance seeking and family accommodation?
How is treatment paced and agreed?
When do you involve partners or family members?
How do you handle co-occurring depression, trauma, substance use, autism, ADHD, eating problems, or other relevant conditions?
How do you coordinate with medication prescribers when needed?
What should a partner do if there is a safety concern?

The goal is not to find someone who gives the exact answer this book gives. It is to find qualified care that can explain its reasoning clearly.

What Evidence-Based Care Means Here

NICE recommends cognitive behavioral therapy including ERP for adults with OCD at different levels of functional impairment and includes SSRIs among treatment options. It also says that a family member may be involved as a co-therapist in ERP when appropriate and acceptable, and that treatment plans should help family members reduce involvement in compulsions, avoidance, or reassurance seeking sensitively and supportively. (National Institute for Health and Care Excellence, 2005)

NHS guidance likewise describes CBT with ERP as the usual talking therapy for OCD and SSRIs as the main medication class used. (NHS, 2023)

These are broad clinical recommendations. An individual assessment determines what is appropriate for a particular person.

A partner should not use the guidelines as a prescription pad.

If You Are Invited to a Session

Bring a one-page note.

What I currently do

List no more than five accommodations.

1. ____

2. ____

3. ____

4. ____

5. ____

What happens when I stop

Describe observable reactions without diagnosis.

Example: "The question repeats ten to fifteen times, the conversation becomes an argument, and I usually answer again."

Example: "My partner becomes upset and cleans the item independently."

Example: "The children are asked instead."

____

What I want help with

Choose two.

How to respond to repeated reassurance.

Which accommodation to target first.

How to distinguish safety from checking.

How to stop debating.

How to protect sleep.

How to keep children out of rituals.

How to handle treatment discussions at home.

How to support ERP without designing it.

How to respond when the person refuses the planned strategy.

Other: ____

_

Ask for the Partner Role in Plain Language

At the end of the session, you should be able to complete this table.

Situation	What the clinician wants me to do	What I should not do
Reassurance request		
Delegated check		
Planned exposure		
Distress spike		
Lapse		
Safety concern		

If the role is unclear, ask again.

"Should I answer a first practical question?"

"Do you want me to use a particular phrase?"

"Am I supposed to participate in this exposure or simply stop accommodating?"

"What counts as new safety information?"

"What do I do if I am too tired or unavailable?"

"How often should we review this at home?"

Specific instructions reduce relationship conflict because the partner is not making clinical policy in real time.

Decide How Much Treatment Talk Comes Home

Treatment can improve when families understand the plan. Relationships can deteriorate when every hour becomes treatment review.

Agree on a home structure.

Treatment check-in frequency: ______________________________

Maximum time: ______________________________

Topics that belong in the check-in: ______________________________

Topics that stay with the clinician: ______________________________

Times when treatment talk is off-limits unless urgent: ______________

For example: fifteen minutes after dinner three nights a week, with no ERP review in bed.

The exact structure is a relationship choice, not a research-based dose.

Privacy Agreement

Your partner's treatment information belongs to them.

Agree on what they want shared.

I may know: ______________________________

I do not need to know: ______________________________

Clinician may contact me about: ______________________________

I may contact clinician about: ______________________________

Emergency exception: ______________________________

Do not assume that being married gives you access to all clinical information.

Likewise, you are allowed to give a clinician information about your own experience where lawful, but the clinician may be unable to disclose treatment information in return.

If You Disagree With the Clinician

A partner may believe the therapist is asking for too much or too little accommodation change.

Start with clarification.

"Can you explain the purpose of this partner task?"

"How does this fit the treatment plan?"

"What risks or exceptions should we know?"

"Is there a smaller role I can take?"

If you still do not consent to your role, say so.

"I understand the rationale. I am not willing to be the person who runs that exposure."

You are not refusing your partner's right to treatment. You are defining your participation.

If a clinician recommends something that appears unsafe, outside their scope, coercive, or inconsistent with appropriate care, seek a second professional opinion where possible.

If Your Partner Does Not Want You in Treatment

Respect that boundary unless safety or legal obligations require action.

You can still change your own accommodation.

You can still seek your own therapy or support.

You can still set household limits.

You can still say, "I do not need to know what you discuss in therapy. I do need a workable agreement about repeated checking in the house."

Treatment privacy does not cancel relationship boundaries.

Treatment Conversation for a Partner Who Is Refusing Help

Use this page to prepare one conversation rather than many.

What I observe: ____

How it affects shared life: ____________________________________

What I am asking: ____

What practical help I can offer: ______________________________

What I will not take over: ____________________________________

What boundary applies whether treatment happens or not: ____________

Example:

"I've noticed we spend most evenings checking contamination questions and that I have stopped having friends over. I want us to get help from someone experienced with OCD. I can help find three options and attend a first appointment if you want. I will not choose treatment for you. Whether you go or not, I am no longer asking visitors to follow the extra washing rule."

The conversation does not require agreement to be complete.

Review After a Month

If treatment is under way, ask:

Is my role clearer?
Am I doing less treatment work than my partner?
Have accommodations been named specifically?
Are we protecting non-treatment time?
Do we know what to do with real safety concerns?
Am I respecting privacy?
Do I need my own support?

If the answers are mostly no, a partner session or treatment-plan clarification may be useful.

The best partner role is usually smaller, clearer, and more ordinary than the role fear first assigns.

Appendix E: Safety and Escalation Planning Sheet

This appendix is intentionally more conservative than the rest of the book. A repeated reassurance question and a real emergency can involve the same subject. The difference may depend on facts a general book cannot see.

Complete this page during a calm period. Use services and procedures that apply where you live.

Your Safety Contacts

Local emergency number: ____

Primary medical clinician: ____

Mental-health clinician or service: _________________________________

Pharmacy or medication contact: ____________________________________

Poison or toxicology advice service, if available: ____________________

Crisis service: ____

Domestic-abuse or violence support: _________________________________

Trusted person who can help in a crisis: ____________________________

Child/dependent support contact, if relevant: _______________________

Do not leave these blank if you already know you may need them. A crisis is a poor time to search for basic numbers.

The Five-Question Safety Screen

Before applying an accommodation limit to an urgent request, ask:

1. Is there new objective information?

Examples include an alarm, smoke, a gas odor, a visible injury, a medication error, a credible threat, a new severe symptom, a missing child, an actual collision, or a professional warning.

Your notes:

---

2. Is there a recognized safety procedure?

Examples include a fire-evacuation plan, medical advice, a prescribed medication process, workplace procedure, child-safety rule, or traffic law.

Your notes:

---

3. Has the appropriate step already been completed?

An ordinary first check is different from repeating a completed check until it feels certain.

Your notes:

---

4. Would I respond the same way if OCD were not part of the picture?

This question helps guard against both dismissing a real hazard and treating anxiety itself as proof of danger.

Your notes:

---

5. Does this require professional judgment?

If you are being asked to decide whether a person is medically safe, suicidal, violent, legally responsible, fit to drive, or correctly medicated, the answer may belong with a professional or emergency service.

Your notes:

Emergency Versus Reassurance Examples

These examples illustrate distinctions. They are not diagnostic rules.

Situation	Treat first as	Why
Smoke alarm sounding	Real safety event	Objective new information
Asking for the tenth time whether the stove is off after one normal check, no new information	Possible checking loop	Repetition after ordinary procedure
New medication dose accidentally taken twice	Medical issue	Potential dosing risk
Repeated question about whether a correctly taken prescribed dose was "really safe" after professional advice	Possible reassurance loop	Same information being rechecked

Situation	Treat first as	Why
Credible statement of intent to harm self	Crisis concern	Requires professional assessment
Repeated request to certify "I would never hurt myself" where symptom history is OCD, but no current risk assessment exists	Needs careful distinction	Partner should not diagnose risk from a script
Door is actually found open	Real security issue	Material change
Hypothetical "what if the lock failed even though it is visibly locked?"	Possible certainty loop	New hypothetical, not new event

When in doubt about significant risk, choose the safer route and seek appropriate professional guidance.

Medical Plan

If your partner has a recurring health concern that attracts reassurance, ask a clinician, with your partner's consent, whether there is an ordinary plan.

What symptoms or changes require medical contact: ____________________

What can be monitored routinely: ____________________

What should not be repeatedly checked: ____________________

Who decides if uncertain: ____________________

Where the written plan is kept: ____________________

Do not invent red flags from internet searches.

Medication Plan

Current medication list kept at: ____________________

Prescriber: ____________________

Pharmacy: ____________________

What to do if a dose may have been missed: ______________________________

What to do if a dose may have been repeated: ______________________________

What to do about side effects: ____

Fill these lines from professional guidance, not memory.

The partner's safety role is to use the correct channel, not to become the medication authority.

Self-Harm and Suicide Concern

Write the action you will take if your partner says they intend to harm themselves, cannot stay safe, or has a plan.

My first action: ____

Who I will contact: ____

Where I can go if the home is unsafe: __________________________________

Who else needs to know for safety: _____________________________________

Do not promise secrecy around imminent risk.

Do not use "this is probably OCD" as your only assessment.

If intrusive self-harm thoughts are a known OCD symptom, ask the treating clinician how *you* should distinguish the agreed reassurance response from situations requiring immediate assessment.

Violence and Coercion Plan

Answer privately.

Has your partner ever blocked you from leaving a room?

Taken your phone, keys, money, or documents to force compliance?

Threatened you, a child, a pet, or another person?

Destroyed property to make you participate in a ritual?

Threatened self-harm specifically to force a reassurance or checking response?

Monitored your movements in a way that makes you afraid?

Used physical force?

If yes to any, accommodation work should not be treated as a simple communication exercise.

Write a safety plan with qualified help where available.

Safe place I can go: ____________________

Person who knows what is happening: ____________________

Documents or essentials I may need: ____________________

Professional service I can contact: ____________________

Safest way to communicate if monitored: ____________________

Do not announce a boundary in a way that increases danger merely to prove consistency.

Children and Dependents

Who depends on adults in the household: ____________________

Current OCD-related rules affecting them: ____________________

Any repeated washing, checking, confession, reassurance, or avoidance they are required to do: ____________________

Any skin injury, sleep loss, school effect, isolation, fear, or restricted care: ____________________

Adult/professional I can contact if the impact grows: ____________________

A dependent person's welfare can require action before the adults agree about whether a behavior is OCD.

Real Safety Procedure Card

Choose one common safety-themed trigger and define the ordinary response.

Example:

Trigger: leaving home.

Ordinary procedure: last person out locks the door once.

New information that changes the plan: door later observed open, security alert, credible report of entry.

Not new information: "what if the lock did not catch even though we checked?"

Partner response after procedure: "The ordinary lock check is done. I won't repeat it."

Now write yours.

Trigger: ____

Ordinary procedure: ____

New information: ____

Not new information: ____

Partner response: ____

After an Escalation

Once everyone is safe, review the event without deciding that either all future boundaries are dangerous or all future distress should be ignored.

What happened before the escalation?

Was the accommodation target announced?

Was there a real safety signal?

Was there coercion or violence?

Did a child witness or participate?

Did I remain in a situation that felt unsafe because I was trying to hold a limit?

What professional support is needed before trying again?

What should change in the plan?

An escalation is data about safety and capacity. It is not a challenge to become tougher.

Keep the Hierarchy Clear

When competing priorities appear, use this order.

Immediate safety comes before accommodation reduction.

Dependent safety comes before household harmony.

Professional medical or psychiatric judgment comes before partner guesswork.

Shared legal and financial responsibilities come before a self-help rule.

After those are addressed, repeated certainty seeking can return to the accommodation plan.

A good OCD boundary never requires pretending that the real world has no hazards.

It requires using proportionate safety procedures without asking those procedures to produce impossible certainty.

Appendix F: Decision Scenarios and Selected Resources

This appendix gives short partner decisions across common situations. Each scenario uses the same sequence: identify the function, check safety, choose your behavior, keep the relationship issue separate, and use professional help where the decision exceeds your role.

The examples are composites. They are designed to help you think, not to tell you what a real person should do without context.

Scenario One: The Locked Door

Daniel asks Maya whether the front door is locked. Maya was the last person out and remembers locking it.

First ask: she answers, "Yes, I locked it."

Three minutes later Daniel asks whether she pulled the handle.

Maya identifies repetition after an ordinary household procedure. There is no new information. Her response is, "I answered the door question. I'm not doing another check."

Daniel says the neighborhood has had break-ins.

That fact may explain why the theme feels urgent, but it does not automatically create new information about their door. If they want to review their ordinary home-security procedure, they can do it at another time.

Partner principle: a real-world subject can still host a repetitive certainty loop.

Scenario Two: The Door Is Actually Open

The next week, a neighbor texts Maya that the front door appears open.

This is new objective information.

Maya does not refuse to respond because door checking is an accommodation target. The couple follows an appropriate security procedure.

Later, Daniel asks twelve times whether the open door means someone must have entered.

The real event has been handled. The repeated interpretation may become a reassurance loop.

Partner principle: respond to the event, then reassess the process.

Scenario Three: The Relationship Question After a Fight

Grace and Luis have a genuine argument about money. Luis apologizes for making a purchase without discussion. Grace is still angry.

Luis asks, "Does this mean you don't love me?"

Grace does not need to deny her anger.

She says, "I'm angry about the purchase, and I love you. We need to fix the money issue."

Ten minutes later he asks whether she is sure the relationship will survive.

Grace says, "I'm willing to work on the actual money problem. I'm not going to keep guaranteeing the entire future tonight."

Partner principle: real repair and refusal of repeated certainty can occur together.

Scenario Four: A Health Symptom

Priya notices a new symptom she has not had before.

Marcus has learned not to inspect the same stable symptom repeatedly, but this is new.

He does not diagnose it as OCD. Priya uses an appropriate medical channel.

After a clinician gives advice, Priya asks Marcus every half hour whether he thinks the clinician missed something. No new symptom or instruction has appeared.

Marcus says, "We followed the medical plan. If something changes according to the guidance we were given, we'll act. I won't keep reinterpreting it."

Partner principle: medical care first, repeated reassurance second.

Scenario Five: The Child as Checker

Owen asks his daughter whether she saw him turn off the faucet.

She answers yes.

He asks again with more detail.

Nia steps in: "You do not need to answer again. Dad can handle the faucet question with the grown-ups."

Later, Nia talks to Owen privately.

"The kids are not going to be checking witnesses. If you want to discuss how we handle that symptom, we can bring it to treatment."

Partner principle: protect a child from the role without making the child enforce the boundary.

Scenario Six: The Visitor Rule

Caleb wants Simone to ask a friend to change clothes before sitting on the couch.

There is no public-health or medical reason for the request. It is part of a long-standing contamination rule.

Simone told Caleb in advance that she would no longer enforce the clothing rule for visitors.

She says, "I know this is difficult. I'm not asking our guest to change."

Caleb chooses to sit in another room.

Simone does not order him to sit beside the guest as exposure. She continues the visit.

Partner principle: stop enforcing the rule without forcing treatment.

Scenario Seven: Therapy Homework

Jonah tells Elena that his therapist wants him to send a routine email without repeated rereading.

He asks Elena to watch him do it and tell him whether he resisted correctly.

Elena is not sure whether the clinician intended her to participate.

She says, "I want to support the plan, but I don't want to grade the homework. Let's write that question down for your therapist."

If the therapist later asks Elena to perform a specific role and both partners agree, the role can change.

Partner principle: uncertainty about treatment roles belongs with the treating clinician.

Scenario Eight: Refusing Treatment

Amir says he does not want therapy.

Tessa has already explained why she thinks specialist OCD care would help. Repeating the sales pitch has become a fight.

She says, "Treatment is your choice. I am not going to keep persuading you. I am also not going back into the apartment to do the second stove check."

She starts individual support for herself and reviews the effect of OCD on sleep and work.

Partner principle: another adult owns treatment consent; you own your participation.

Scenario Nine: A Real Relationship Boundary

Elena discovers that Jonah has used shared savings without agreement.

Jonah begins asking whether the mistake proves he is a terrible person.

Elena refuses the moral reassurance loop but does not let the financial issue disappear.

"I won't decide your character for you. We do need to restore the money and agree on how spending works."

Partner principle: an OCD loop can occur around a real problem; address both at the correct level.

Scenario Ten: Threat After a Limit

Marcus refuses an extra contamination ritual. Priya threatens to smash his laptop if he leaves the room.

Marcus does not treat the threat as a sign that he should hold the accommodation boundary more firmly.

He prioritizes safety, leaves the situation if safe to do so, and seeks appropriate help.

The future accommodation plan may need professional support and a broader relationship-safety assessment.

Partner principle: violence and coercion override a workbook exercise.

Scenario Eleven: A Bad Day in Treatment

Maya's partner has been using a reassurance-reduction plan successfully for weeks. After a stressful family event, the questions return intensely.

Maya is tempted to answer everything "just tonight."

Instead she holds the two established limits she knows best and drops the idea of adding any new target.

She offers practical care: dinner, quiet company, help contacting the clinician if wanted.

Partner principle: a flare-up calls for maintenance, not panic or expansion.

Scenario Twelve: The Partner Is the One Who Needs a Bigger Change

Simone realizes that she has restored several routines, but she is still afraid to leave Caleb alone for an evening because he may call repeatedly.

There is no current safety reason she must stay available.

She schedules one evening with a friend, tells Caleb she will not answer nonurgent reassurance messages, and keeps an emergency contact route.

The outing is not an exposure she is administering to Caleb. It is part of Simone's ordinary life.

Partner principle: restoration is not a bonus after symptom improvement. It is part of the partner's boundary work.

Scenario Thirteen: The Answer Is Actually Unknown

Nia asks Owen whether he mailed an important form. Owen genuinely cannot remember.

Nia does not say, "I won't reassure you," because there is a practical task with real consequences.

They check the tracking system once.

After confirming delivery, Owen asks whether the tracking system could be wrong.

Nia says, "The practical issue is resolved. I'm not going to keep proving the delivery."

Partner principle: solve the real task once, then stop converting residual uncertainty into more checking.

Scenario Fourteen: The First Reassurance Is Also a Ritual

Luis asks Grace, "Tell me I'm not dangerous."

Grace knows from their clinician-guided plan that this specific question is an established compulsion and that the agreed response is not to provide even a first moral verdict.

She says, "I know the urge is strong. I'm using the response we agreed with your therapist."

Partner principle: the book's general "ordinary first answer" distinction does not override an individualized treatment plan.

Scenario Fifteen: No Diagnosis Yet

A reader suspects their partner has OCD because of repeated checking and reassurance, but the partner has never been assessed.

The reader should not announce a diagnosis.

They can still set ordinary boundaries.

"I don't want to answer the same question ten times."

"I can't keep losing sleep to repeated checking."

"I think these patterns deserve professional assessment."

Partner principle: a partner limit does not require a home diagnosis.

Selected High-Quality Resources

Use resources to support accurate understanding, not to build a larger reassurance library.

International OCD Foundation

The International OCD Foundation publishes educational material on OCD, ERP, family accommodation, and finding help. Its family guidance is especially relevant to limits, reassurance, routines, and the effect of OCD on family life.

Useful for: plain-language family education, clinician directories in available regions, conferences, support information, and condition-specific articles.

Caution: provider directories indicate self-reported professional information and availability can change. A listing is not a guarantee of fit.

NICE Clinical Guideline CG31

The National Institute for Health and Care Excellence guideline covers recognition and treatment of OCD and body dysmorphic disorder. Its recommendations address family involvement, CBT including ERP, medication options, and reducing family participation in compulsions, avoidance, and reassurance seeking.

Useful for: understanding broad evidence-based treatment recommendations and the intended role of families and carers.

Caution: the guideline was published in 2005, last reviewed in 2024, and is being updated in areas identified by NICE. Current clinical decisions should use up-to-date professional guidance.

NHS OCD Information

The NHS describes OCD symptoms and treatment in accessible language, including CBT with ERP and SSRIs.

Useful for: basic treatment overview and medication safety language.

Caution: NHS service pathways are specific to the United Kingdom. Readers elsewhere should use local health systems.

Peer-Reviewed Family Accommodation Research

The research base includes reviews and meta-analyses showing that family accommodation is common and moderately associated with OCD severity, as well as treatment studies examining family involvement.

Useful for: understanding why accommodation belongs in the clinical conversation.

Caution: association is not simple proof that family accommodation causes symptom severity. Studies vary in population, measurement, and design.

How to Find an OCD-Informed Clinician

A useful clinician should be able to explain how they assess OCD and how they treat it.

Questions to ask:

"How often do you treat OCD?"

"How do you use CBT and ERP?"

"How do you distinguish exposure from reassurance or ritual?"

"How do you involve partners when family accommodation is significant?"

"What happens if the person refuses or cannot tolerate ERP?"

"How do you address safety concerns separately from OCD fears?"

"How do you coordinate care for medication or co-occurring conditions?"

You do not need the clinician to use the exact language of this book.

You need them to have a coherent, evidence-based treatment approach and to explain partner involvement clearly.

How to Use Online Communities

Online communities can help partners hear experiences they do not encounter elsewhere. They can also spread advice that is too absolute for a particular situation.

Use communities for perspective and peer connection.

Do not use anonymous comments as medical instructions.

Be cautious with claims such as:

"Never reassure, no matter what."

"All relationship doubt is ROCD."

"If they get angry, that means the boundary is working."

"ERP always means doing the worst fear."

"Medication never works."

"Medication is the only thing that works."

"Your partner is manipulating you."

"Your partner cannot help any of their behavior because it is OCD."

Real couples are more complicated than slogans.

A Resource Quality Check

Before relying on a resource, ask:

Who created it?

What qualifications or organization stand behind it?

Does it distinguish research from opinion?

Does it describe limits and uncertainty?

Does it separate emergency guidance from self-help?

Does it avoid promising a cure?

Does it recommend individualized professional care where appropriate?

Does it treat the person with OCD as an adult with autonomy?

Does it protect partners and children from being turned into treatment instruments?

A resource does not need to be academic to be useful. It should be transparent about what kind of authority it has.

When to Stop Researching

Partners often research because knowledge is one of the few things they can control.

There is a point where more reading becomes another way to postpone a decision.

You probably have enough information to act on your side when you can answer these questions:

What is family accommodation?

Which two accommodations do I perform most often?

What is my first partner limit?

What ordinary life do I want to restore?

What safety concerns require professional help?

What is my treatment role, if any?

What happens if my partner refuses treatment?

If you can answer those, close the tabs.

Use the plan.

Research again when a genuinely new question appears.

Fast Decision Guide for Live Moments

This guide is for the moment when you do not have time to reread a chapter. Find the closest pattern, then check safety before using the response.

Someone asks the same question again

Ask yourself: Did I already provide the ordinary information I have? Is there new information, or only a new version of the doubt?

If there is no new information, use a process response.

"I answered once. I don't have more certainty to add."

Then return to ordinary activity.

If there is new information, deal with the new fact once.

Someone asks you to check for them

Ask: Is this normally my responsibility? Has the ordinary check already been completed? Is the request transferring responsibility for uncertainty to me?

If the task is theirs and already complete, decline the delegated check.

"I'm not doing another check. The ordinary one is done."

If the task is genuinely yours, complete the ordinary task without adding ritual layers.

Someone asks you to witness a check

Watching can become certification.

Ask whether your presence is serving safety or certainty.

If it is certainty:

"I won't be the witness for the check."

If a professional treatment plan asks you to participate in a specific way, follow that plan instead.

Someone asks for a photograph

A photograph can be a practical record or a checking object.

Ask how it will be used.

If the photograph is repeatedly inspected for certainty, stop producing it.

"I won't take another photo for checking."

If the photograph has a legitimate practical purpose, keep that purpose separate.

A household rule affects you

Ask whether the rule is a shared preference, a real safety requirement, an access need, or a fear-driven ritual rule.

If it is a clear accommodation target:

"I won't follow that extra rule with my own things."

Do not force your partner to change their private ritual as a condition of your boundary.

A household rule affects children

Move the child's role out first.

"The kids are not going to do the checking or reassurance."

Then seek professional help if the impact on the child is significant or the adults cannot agree on a safe standard.

Your partner says the boundary is cruel

Do not prove your goodness.

Ask what specifically felt cruel.

If your tone or timing was poor, repair it.

"I was sharp. I am sorry. I still won't repeat the check."

If the objection is that any refusal is cruel, state your position once and stop debating.

Your partner says the fear is different this time

Look for a material external change.

A new hypothetical is not automatically new information.

"I hear the new angle. I don't see new practical information, so my response is the same."

If there is a real change, respond to it.

You are not sure whether it is OCD

Do not force the label.

Set a boundary you can justify without diagnosis.

"I can't spend another hour on this question."

"I won't inspect the door again."

"I think we need professional assessment before we keep deciding this at home."

The request is about medication

Do not guess.

Use the prescriber, pharmacist, poison service, or appropriate medical contact.

After the real medication question is resolved, you can decline repeated certainty checks.

The request is about a health symptom

New, significant, or changing symptoms use ordinary medical channels.

Stable information already appropriately assessed may later become a reassurance target.

Do not make the medical judgment solely to avoid accommodation.

The request is about whether your partner is dangerous

Do not become the moral-certainty provider.

Also do not ignore credible risk.

If there is stated intent, plan, inability to stay safe, escalating violence, or another concrete concern, seek professional or emergency help.

If the question is an established reassurance compulsion under a treatment plan, use the agreed response.

Your partner refuses treatment

Stop daily persuasion.

Make one clear invitation.

Set your own accommodation limits.

Seek your own support.

Review what you need for the relationship to remain workable.

Your partner is in treatment and wants you involved

Ask for the exact treatment role.

Do not assume that knowing about ERP means you should design it.

A useful role can be small: one reassurance response, one accommodation target, one agreed participation task.

Your partner is in treatment and does not want you involved

Respect treatment privacy.

Keep boundaries around your own behavior.

"I do not need treatment details. I do need us to agree on what happens with repeated checking at home."

You gave reassurance after planning not to

Stop at the next opportunity.

"I got pulled back into answering. I'm not going to continue."

Do not demand that your partner process your lapse.

Review privately why it happened.

You were rude while holding a limit

Repair the rudeness.

Do not automatically reverse the boundary.

"I should not have mocked you. I'm sorry. I'm still not doing the extra check."

Your partner follows you after you end the conversation

State the exit once.

"I am taking a break from this conversation."

If they block your movement, take your phone, threaten you, or make you afraid, treat it as a safety problem.

A relative wants to reassure because it seems kind

Do not shame them.

Explain the narrow pattern if disclosure is appropriate.

"One normal answer is fine. Please don't keep repeating the same certainty."

If diagnostic privacy matters, simply tell them they do not have to keep answering.

You are exhausted

Choose the smallest limit you can actually keep.

"I am going to sleep. I won't answer repeated questions tonight."

If there is a real emergency, use the safety plan.

Do not launch a new high-difficulty accommodation target when you have no capacity to handle the conversation.

You feel resentful

Do not use the live reassurance request to settle the history of the relationship.

Hold the specific limit.

Schedule the larger conversation.

"We need to talk about how much this has taken from me. I don't want to do that while we're arguing about this check."

Your partner is improving and you want to monitor it

Do less.

Notice your own accommodation, ordinary life, and treatment-role boundaries.

Let clinical symptom tracking belong to treatment unless you have an agreed role.

A flare-up happens

Return to established limits.

Do not add new targets.

Do not assume you are back at the beginning.

Protect safety and ordinary life.

Encourage return to professional support where appropriate.

You are considering leaving the relationship

Do not make the decision into an anti-OCD tactic.

Get direct support around safety, finances, housing, children, legal issues, and relationship values as relevant.

Your partner's diagnosis does not decide whether you must stay.

You want one sentence to remember

Use this:

Support the person. Do not do the compulsion's job.

Then ask what the compulsion's job would be in this moment: certainty, checking, avoidance, ritual completion, responsibility transfer, or household control.

If the answer is clear and safety is addressed, choose your side of the line.

Canonical Glossary

family accommodation: a family member's participation in compulsions, reassurance, avoidance, or routine changes made in response to OCD symptoms.

reassurance seeking: repeated attempts to obtain certainty or relief from another person about an OCD-related doubt.

delegated checking: asking another person to perform or certify a check so responsibility for uncertainty is transferred.

OCD rule: a household or relationship rule whose main function is to reduce OCD-related distress or uncertainty.

Support Pivot: the four-step partner response: notice the pattern, meet the person, decline the accommodation, return the next choice.

process not proof: responding to the reassurance process rather than debating whether the feared content is true.

accommodation target: one specific accommodating behavior selected for reduction.

graded reduction: reducing accommodation in planned steps rather than attempting to stop every behavior at once.

partner limit: a clear statement of what the partner will or will not do, framed around the partner's own behavior.

ordinary life: household, relationship, work, sleep, social, and personal activities chosen for their own value rather than organized around OCD.

treatment role: the limited, consent-based way a partner participates in professional OCD treatment.

safety screen: a check for genuine medical, violence, self-harm, dependent-safety, or emergency concerns before treating a request as an OCD loop.

recovery marker: a practical sign such as less accommodation, more responsibility, more flexibility, or more ordinary activity.

restoration target: the ordinary-life activity, choice, or relationship function that an accommodation reduction is meant to restore.

broken-record response: a short boundary sentence repeated without adding new reasons, then followed by disengagement from the loop.

repair window: a later, planned time to discuss tone, conflict, or relationship harm without reopening the content of a reassurance loop.

ordinary standard: the proportionate real-world procedure that would apply if the same task were not being used to obtain extra certainty.

new information: a material external change or credible fact that can alter a real-world safety or practical decision, rather than a new hypothetical version of the same fear.

Use these terms consistently when talking with a clinician or partner if they are useful. Do not insist that another person adopt the vocabulary before you can set a clear boundary.

Seven-Day Reset When the Household Feels Stuck

Use this reset when you have read a great deal, argued about accommodation, and still do not know what to do first. It deliberately limits activity.

Day One: Stop Changing Things

Do not announce a new boundary.

Record three accommodation interactions only.

Write what you did, not what your partner should have done.

If a safety issue appears, respond to safety as usual.

Day Two: Choose the Lowest-Cost Loop

Pick the interaction that is frequent, specific, and low in genuine safety stakes.

Avoid choosing the most emotionally loaded topic.

Good first targets are often a repeat answer, a delegated low-risk check, or a small routine modification.

Write one behavioral sentence.

"I will not ____."

Day Three: Write the Support Pivot

Write the four moves in your own words.

Notice: "I think this is ____."

Meet: "I know ____."

Decline: "I won't ____."

Return: "You can ____."

Now shorten the whole thing to one or two sentences.

Say it aloud once.

Day Four: Restore Something Small

Choose a piece of ordinary life that does not require your partner to perform treatment.

Take lunch without reassurance texting.

Go to your class.

Call a friend.

Use a shared room normally.

Go to bed at the planned time.

Do not choose the activity because you expect it to provoke anxiety. Choose it because it belongs in your life.

Day Five: Have the Calm-Period Conversation

If safe and practical, tell your partner what you are changing.

Keep it under five minutes.

Do not present twenty pages of research.

"I've noticed that I answer the same question several times. I'm going to answer once and then stop repeating it. I know this may be hard. I want us to have less of our evening taken by the question."

If they want to discuss the principle, schedule a short time.

If they want to debate the feared content, do not use the policy conversation as another reassurance session.

Day Six: Hold One Live Limit

When the target occurs, use the sentence.

Expect imperfection.

If you give in, stop at the next repetition.

If you become rude, repair later.

If there is real danger, use the safety plan.

Do not add a second target because the first attempt went well.

Day Seven: Review Your Side

Answer five questions.

Did I recognize the pattern?

Did I keep safety separate?

Did I meet the person without certifying the fear?

Did I decline the accommodation clearly?

Did ordinary life continue afterward?

If three of five are yes, you learned something useful.

If none are yes, make the target smaller.

If the week revealed coercion, child impact, medical ambiguity, or a treatment question, shift from self-help to appropriate professional support.

The reset does not promise symptom change in seven days. It gives the partner a week with one job at a time.

Evidence Notes for Readers Who Want the Research

The book's central argument depends on a modest claim: family accommodation is common in OCD, is meaningfully associated with symptom severity, and is important enough that clinical guidance and treatment research address it. The evidence does not justify blaming partners or claiming that accommodation alone causes OCD.

Family Accommodation and Symptom Severity

Strauss, Hale, and Stobie published a 2015 meta-analysis of fourteen studies with 849 participants. They found a significant moderate relationship between family accommodation and OCD symptom severity, with a pooled correlation of .35. The design of the underlying literature did not support a simple causal conclusion. (Strauss et al., 2015)

Wu and colleagues published a larger meta-analysis in 2016 including forty-one studies. They found an overall correlation of .42 between family accommodation and OCD symptom severity. Their review also emphasized measurement differences across studies. (Wu et al., 2016)

Hermida-Barros and colleagues updated the evidence in 2024. Their systematic review and meta-analysis included 108 studies and 8,928 people with OCD. They again found a positive correlation of .42 between family accommodation and OCD severity. They also reported decreases in accommodation across individual and family-focused CBT. Baseline accommodation did not simply predict how much OCD severity changed from before to after treatment. (Hermida-Barros et al., 2024)

Taken together, these studies support attention to accommodation while arguing against a one-cause explanation.

What Accommodation Includes

Research definitions extend beyond reassurance. Reviews describe family participation in rituals, facilitating avoidance, changing routines, and other behaviors that reduce or prevent OCD-related distress. (Albert et al., 2017; Wu et al., 2016)

This broader definition is why the book maps time, space, money, sleep, social life, and household rules rather than focusing only on the sentence "Are you sure?"

Reassurance Seeking

Starcevic and colleagues assessed 140 adults with OCD and found that 67, or 47.9 percent, reported interpersonal reassurance seeking. Reassurance seeking was related to checking but was not treated as identical to checking. (Starcevic et al., 2012)

Salkovskis and Kobori examined self-reported patterns of reassurance seeking. Their participants with OCD described short-term relief after reassurance followed by return of discomfort and renewed reassurance urges. Because the study relied on retrospective self-report, it is best used to understand a pattern rather than as proof that every reassuring exchange produces a fixed outcome. (Salkovskis & Kobori, 2015)

Family Intervention

Thompson-Hollands and colleagues ran a preliminary randomized study with eighteen patient-family pairs. Patients received standard individual ERP, while family members were randomized to receive or not receive a brief two-session intervention targeting accommodation. The family intervention reduced clinician-rated accommodation, and the patient group whose family members received the intervention showed greater OCD symptom reductions in that small study. The sample size and preliminary nature matter. (Thompson-Hollands et al., 2015)

The responsible takeaway is that structured family accommodation work may add value in treatment, not that a partner should reproduce the intervention independently.

Couple-Based Treatment

Abramowitz and colleagues described a couple-based approach designed to enhance ERP for people with OCD in long-term relationships. The approach addresses interpersonal processes and accommodation while preserving ERP as the OCD treatment. The publication includes a program description and case material. (Abramowitz et al., 2013)

This is why the book distinguishes an agreed treatment role from informal partner-led therapy.

Clinical Guidance

NICE guideline CG31 recommends that adults with OCD may receive CBT including ERP and describes SSRIs as a treatment option depending on severity and circumstances. It says family members may be involved in ERP when appropriate and acceptable. It specifically recommends helping family members reduce involvement in compulsive behaviors, avoidance, or reassurance seeking in a sensitive and supportive manner. The guideline was published in 2005, last reviewed in July 2024, and NICE reports an update in progress. (National Institute for Health and Care Excellence, 2005)

The International OCD Foundation's family guidance similarly advises reducing participation in compulsions, setting limits sensitively, preserving ordinary routines, and avoiding endless reassurance debates. (Van Noppen & Pato, 2009)

NHS guidance describes CBT with ERP and medication, usually SSRIs, as the two main treatment routes for OCD. (NHS, 2023)

What the Evidence Does Not Say

The evidence does not say that every act of comfort is accommodation.

It does not say that partners cause OCD.

It does not say that all reassurance should stop immediately.

It does not say that the partner should design ERP.

It does not say that anger after a limit proves the limit is therapeutic.

It does not say that couple therapy alone is an established specific treatment for OCD.

It does not say that a diagnosis explains abuse, coercion, unfairness, or every relationship problem.

The practical strength of the evidence lies in a narrower conclusion: family behavior is part of the OCD context, and reducing symptom-serving participation can be a legitimate treatment and relationship goal when done with appropriate care.

How to Use This Book Later

You do not need to reread the whole book when a familiar pattern returns.

For reassurance, return to Chapters 1, 3, and 5.

For checking, use Chapter 6.

For household rules, use Chapters 7 and 8.

For conflict, use Chapter 9.

For treatment questions, use Chapters 10 and 11.

For relationship-centered doubt, use Chapter 12.

For children and relatives, use Chapter 13.

For your own capacity, use Chapter 14.

For danger, health, or crisis uncertainty, use Chapter 15 and Appendix E.

For maintenance, use Chapter 16 and Appendix C.

The fastest reference is the Support Pivot Script Bank in Appendix B.

Use only the section that matches the current problem. Reading more is not automatically more useful. The book has done its job when you can find one clear next response and then return to ordinary life.

References

Abramowitz, J. S., Baucom, D. H., Wheaton, M. G., Boeding, S., Fabricant, L. E., Paprocki, C., & Fischer, M. S. (2013). Enhancing exposure and response prevention for OCD: A couple-based approach. *Behavior Modification, 37*(2), 189-210. https://doi.org/10.1177/0145445512444596

Albert, U., Baffa, A., & Maina, G. (2017). Family accommodation in adult obsessive-compulsive disorder: Clinical perspectives. *Psychology Research and Behavior Management, 10*, 293-304. https://doi.org/10.2147/PRBM.S124359

Hermida-Barros, L., Primé-Tous, M., García-Delgar, B., Forcadell, E., Lera-Miguel, S., Fernández de la Cruz, L., Vieta, E., Radua, J., Lázaro, L., & Fullana, M. A. (2024). Family accommodation in obsessive-compulsive disorder: An updated systematic review and meta-analysis. *Neuroscience & Biobehavioral Reviews, 161*, 105678. https://doi.org/10.1016/j.neubiorev.2024.105678

National Institute for Health and Care Excellence. (2005). *Obsessive-compulsive disorder and body dysmorphic disorder: Treatment (Clinical guideline CG31).* https://www.nice.org.uk/guidance/cg31

NHS. (2023). *Treatment: Obsessive compulsive disorder (OCD).* https://www.nhs.uk/mental-health/conditions/obsessive-compulsive-disorder-ocd/treatment/

Pellegrini, L., Maietti, E., Rucci, P., Casadei, G., Maina, G., Fineberg, N. A., & Albert, U. (2020). Suicide attempts and suicidal ideation in patients with obsessive-compulsive disorder: A systematic review and meta-analysis. *Journal of Affective Disorders, 276*, 1001-1021. https://doi.org/10.1016/j.jad.2020.07.115

Salkovskis, P. M., & Kobori, O. (2015). Reassuringly calm? Self-reported patterns of responses to reassurance seeking in obsessive compulsive disorder. *Journal of Behavior Therapy and Experimental Psychiatry, 49*(Pt B), 203-208. https://doi.org/10.1016/j.jbtep.2015.09.002

Starcevic, V., Berle, D., Brakoulias, V., Sammut, P., Moses, K., Milicevic, D., & Hannan, A. (2012). Interpersonal reassurance seeking in obsessive-compulsive disorder and its relationship with checking compulsions. *Psychiatry Research, 200*(2-3), 560-567. https://doi.org/10.1016/j.psychres.2012.06.037

Strauss, C., Hale, L., & Stobie, B. (2015). A meta-analytic review of the relationship between family accommodation and OCD symptom severity. *Journal of Anxiety Disorders, 33*, 95-102. https://doi.org/10.1016/j.janxdis.2015.05.006

Thompson-Hollands, J., Abramovitch, A., Tompson, M. C., & Barlow, D. H. (2015). A randomized clinical trial of a brief family intervention to reduce accommodation in obsessive-compulsive disorder: A preliminary study. *Behavior Therapy, 46*(2), 218-229. https://doi.org/10.1016/j.beth.2014.11.001

Van Noppen, B., & Pato, M. (2009). *Living with someone who has OCD: Guidelines for family members.* International OCD Foundation. https://iocdf.org/expert-opinions/expert-opinion-family-guidelines/

Wu, M. S., McGuire, J. F., Martino, C., Phares, V., Selles, R. R., & Storch, E. A. (2016). A meta-analysis of family accommodation and OCD symptom severity. *Clinical Psychology Review, 45*, 34-44. https://doi.org/10.1016/j.cpr.2016.03.003

About the Author

Ruby Virginia Barman writes practical mental-health education for adults who want clear language, usable structure, and careful limits around what a book can claim. Her work emphasizes behavior readers can observe, questions they can bring to qualified professionals, and tools that do not pretend to replace individualized care. No professional license or clinical practice is claimed in this book.

www.ingramcontent.com/pod-product-compliance
Lightning Source LLC
LaVergne TN
LVHW060546061126
851857LV00017B/1919
* 9 7 8 1 9 1 1 8 3 8 4 3 2 *